Survival Guide for Coaching Youth Soccer

Lindsey Blom
Tim Blom

Human Kinetics

Library of Congress Cataloging-in-Publication Data

Blom, Lindsey, 1977-
  Survival guide for coaching youth soccer / Lindsey Blom, Timothy Blom.
    p. cm.
  ISBN-13: 978-0-7360-7732-3 (soft cover)
  ISBN-10: 0-7360-7732-4 (soft cover)
  1. Soccer for children--Coaching. 2. Soccer--Coaching. I. Blom, Timothy, 1976- II. Title.
  GV943.8.B56 2009
  796.33407'7--dc22
                                2009001190

ISBN-10: 0-7360-7732-4 (print)   ISBN-10: 0-7360-8439-8 (Adobe PDF)
ISBN-13: 978-0-7360-7732-3 (print)   ISBN-13: 978-0-7360-8439-0 (Adobe PDF)

Acquisitions Editor: Tom Heine; **Developmental Editor:** Heather Healy; **Assistant Editor:** Carla Zych; **Copyeditor:** Patricia MacDonald; **Proofreader:** Jim Burns; **Permission Manager:** Martha Gullo; **Graphic Designer:** Nancy Rasmus; **Graphic Artist:** Julie L. Denzer; **Cover Designer:** Keith Blomberg; **Photographer (interior):** Neil Bernstein; **Visual Production Assistant:** Joyce Brumfield; **Photo Production Manager:** Jason Allen; **Art Manager:** Kelly Hendren; **Associate Art Manager:** Alan L. Wilborn; **Illustrator:** Tim Brummett; **Printer:** United Graphics

We thank the Dynamo FC Soccer Club in Indianapolis, Indiana, for assistance in providing the location for the photo shoot for this book.

Human Kinetics books are available at special discounts for bulk purchase. Special editions or book excerpts can also be created to specification. For details, contact the Special Sales Manager at Human Kinetics.

Printed in the United States of America   10 9 8 7 6 5 4 3 2 1

The paper in this book is certified under a sustainable forestry program.

Human Kinetics
Web site: www.HumanKinetics.com

United States: Human Kinetics
P.O. Box 5076
Champaign, IL 61825-5076
800-747-4457
e-mail: humank@hkusa.com

Canada: Human Kinetics
475 Devonshire Road Unit 100
Windsor, ON N8Y 2L5
800-465-7301 (in Canada only)
e-mail: info@hkcanada.com

Europe: Human Kinetics
107 Bradford Road
Stanningley
Leeds LS28 6AT, United Kingdom
+44 (0) 113 255 5665
e-mail: hk@hkeurope.com

Australia: Human Kinetics
57A Price Avenue
Lower Mitcham, South Australia 5062
08 8372 0999
e-mail: info@hkaustralia.com

New Zealand: Human Kinetics
Division of Sports Distributors NZ Ltd.
P.O. Box 300 226 Albany
North Shore City
Auckland
0064 9 448 1207
e-mail: info@humankinetics.co.nz

This book is dedicated to Sallie Ryan, Scot Jones, Richard Craig, Bob Ravensberg, Mike Blom, and Bill Grossman—and to parents everywhere who step up to coach, assist, manage, carpool, slice oranges, and give their time and energy to introduce kids to the greatest sport in the world.

 # Contents

🌐 Drill Finder

Drill Title	Skill Warm-Up	Skill Training	Team Training	Games	Fun Competition	Pregame Warm-Up	Dribbling	Passing	Receiving	Shooting	Defending	Goalkeeping	Restarts	Heading	Page
Ball hog	✔	✔					✔								53
Traffic cop	✔	✔				✔	✔								54
Sharks and minnows	✔	✔		✔			✔								55
Obstacle course	✔	✔			✔		✔								56
Knockout	✔	✔			✔		✔								57
Mirror mirror		✔					✔								58
Father time		✔					✔								59
Intersection		✔				✔	✔								60
Gates		✔	✔				✔				✔				61
Individual attacking scrimmage		✔	✔				✔	✔	✔	✔	✔	✔			62
Marbles	✔	✔					✔								81
Tunnel passing	✔	✔				✔		✔	✔						82
Circle passing	✔	✔				✔		✔	✔						83
No-hand catch	✔	✔				✔		✔	✔						84
Monkey in the middle	✔	✔				✔		✔	✔		✔				86
Add-on		✔				✔		✔	✔						87
Blackjack (21)			✔					✔	✔		✔				89
Possession grids			✔					✔	✔		✔				90
Corners			✔					✔	✔		✔				91
Half in, half out			✔					✔	✔		✔				92
Ping-ping	✔	✔								✔	✔				105
Space invaders	✔	✔									✔				106
Check, pass, shoot		✔				✔	✔	✔	✔			✔			107
Power-finesse		✔		✔						✔		✔			108
Everybody keeps		✔		✔						✔		✔			109
Money ball		✔	✔	✔					✔	✔		✔			110

Drill Title	Purpose or Practice part						Skill								Page
	Skill Warm-Up	Skill Training	Team Training	Games	Fun Competition	Pregame Warm-Up	Dribbling	Passing	Receiving	Shooting	Defending	Goalkeeping	Restarts	Heading	
Battle ball		✔	✔		✔					✔		✔			112
World cup			✔		✔		✔	✔	✔	✔	✔	✔			113
Numbers			✔		✔		✔			✔	✔				114
Dog owns the yard			✔	✔	✔		✔	✔	✔	✔	✔	✔			116
Puppet master	✔										✔				129
Shadow defender	✔	✔					✔				✔				130
First-defender warm-up	✔	✔				✔	✔	✔	✔		✔				131
Protect this house		✔			✔		✔	✔			✔				132
Defensive driving lane		✔	✔				✔	✔	✔		✔				133
1v1 to goal		✔	✔			✔	✔	✔	✔	✔	✔	✔			134
Race to the ball		✔				✔	✔			✔	✔				135
Defend the line		✔					✔	✔	✔		✔				136
Turnover			✔	✔			✔	✔	✔	✔	✔	✔			137
Shadow scrimmage				✔			✔	✔	✔	✔	✔	✔			138
Bounce and catch	✔					✔						✔			153
Ball work	✔					✔						✔			154
Sit, throw, jump, catch	✔					✔						✔			155
Crunch and catch	✔					✔						✔			156
Partner pride	✔					✔						✔			158
Two servers	✔					✔						✔			160
Attack the ball	✔	✔					✔					✔			161
Long kicks and throws		✔										✔			162
1v1		✔										✔			163
Circle catches			✔				✔					✔			164
Partner throws	✔	✔							✔				✔		180

(continued)

Drill Finder, *(continued)*

Drill Title	Skill Warm-Up	Skill Training	Team Training	Games	Fun Competition	Pregame Warm-Up	Dribbling	Passing	Receiving	Shooting	Defending	Goalkeeping	Restarts	Heading	Page
	Purpose or Practice part						**Skill**								
Throw to me	✔	✔							✔		✔		✔		181
Heading basics	✔	✔												✔	182
PKs	✔	✔										✔	✔		184
Circle heading		✔												✔	185
Goal clearances		✔						✔	✔				✔		186
Finding a target		✔						✔	✔				✔		187
Basic corner		✔	✔					✔	✔	✔	✔	✔	✔	✔	188
Short corner		✔	✔					✔	✔	✔	✔	✔	✔	✔	189
Basic free kicks		✔	✔					✔	✔	✔	✔	✔	✔	✔	190

 Preface

You could have been put in charge of the orange slices or maybe putting the drink boxes on ice. You'd have been more than happy setting up the phone tree. But, no, somehow you ended up as the head coach. Now your job is to organize eight rambunctious 5- and 6-year-olds—who have as much soccer experience as you do—into a team and quickly. We know what you're thinking: *What did I get myself into? What will I do with Shy Sammy, who doesn't really want to play? What will I do with Chatty Cathy and her loud mother? How will I handle Tiny Tyler, who is afraid of the ball and nimbly darts out of the way when it is near?*

Many helpful people like you volunteer to ensure that the kids have a chance to play. Most of these volunteers feel overwhelmed and unprepared for the task; your feelings are very normal. This book is the perfect guide for helping you survive the chaos of coaching recreational youth soccer. It will help you, the first-time coach, teach the game of soccer in a fun way while helping young players learn basic skills and develop a love for the game. We will be right by your side throughout the season, preparing you for the unexpected and giving you specific instructions to help you stay one step ahead of the kids. We'll take you from the preseason parent meeting to the end-of-season party and of course help you with the really important stuff—the practices and games. You can do this! (You might even enjoy it.)

To help you survive the season, we provide information on the following topics in a manner that is easy to follow. Most of the information is intended for coaching beginning youth soccer players, approximately 5 to 10 years of age. However, we have included suggestions on how to adapt many of the drills and concepts to meet the needs of older or more advanced players.

- **Teaching the rules and positions.** What is offside? How many players play at one time? (Chapter 1 provides all the information you need.)

- **Running effective practices.** What am I supposed to do at practice? How am I ever going to get these kids to listen to me? (See chapter 2 to learn more about planning fun and effective practices.)

- **Teaching individual and team skills.** How do I get the kids to dribble with their feet instead of their hands? How do I explain how to shoot the ball when I don't even know how to kick a soccer ball without using my toe? (Chapters 3 through 8 will help you and your players understand the basics.)

- **Managing games.** Where do I play Dandelion Dana? How do I get Ready Robbie to come out of the game when it is his turn to sub? (In chapters 9 through 11, you will learn how to get your group to play like a team, how to coach games with confidence, and how to manage all the off-field issues that come with coaching youth soccer.)

Each of the skills chapters include 10 drills that will help you teach the basic skills of soccer. The drills were selected based on the five parts of practice (discussed in chapter 2), so you will know how to use the drills and can organize complete practices. In each drill, you will find a clear explanation of how to run the drill, a list of the equipment you will need, and information about how to set up the playing area. For the equipment, we list only the number of balls used in the drill at one time; however, we recommend having several balls nearby so you can send a new ball into the playing area if one is knocked out. This way you can keep play going, and players will spend less time standing around waiting for someone to retrieve a ball. As you set up boundaries for the playing areas, consider placing cones every 3 to 5 yards or meters (if you are lucky enough to have this many cones). Many of the drills also include coaching points to help your players benefit from them as well as modifications to help you change things up when needed.

Whether you have the time and energy to carefully plan every last detail or you need a quick refresher and some drills as you pull up to the field, *Survival Guide for Coaching Youth Soccer* should give you the confidence and support to lead your team. We hope you'll enjoy this book. More important, we hope this book will help you enjoy your coaching experience. It was written with the same philosophy we use as coaches: Soccer equals fun. When practice plans seem to fall apart or game-day strategies appear to fail, remember that if the kids are having fun, then you are doing a great job!

⚽ Acknowledgements

We met on a soccer field in Statesboro, Georgia, twelve years ago. A few years later we were married, and thirteen of the fourteen members of our wedding party were either family members or teammates. God has blessed us through soccer with countless opportunities to be challenged as athletes, to meet and get to know amazing people, and to travel around our country and internationally. The two-year process of creating this book has been another wonderful soccer adventure.

We should first thank all the people that helped to fuel our passion for soccer and brought us from field to field until our paths crossed at Georgia Southern. Our parents, Mike and Rosemary and Becky and Bill, have been our biggest supporters as players, coaches, and now writers. We appreciate their unconditional love. Our brothers and sisters have been a big inspiration, with their constant check-ins to be sure that we were meeting our deadlines! Makenzie has unknowingly been a great sport throughout this process, even when she climbed into our laps and closed the computer. Little does she know that her future coaches may read this book.

We certainly must thank our former coaches and clubs; our experiences with them shaped our coaching philosophy and nurtured our love for the game. A huge thank you goes out to Craig Fedor, Frank Dixon, Phil Neddo, Scott Emison, Tom Norton, and Kevin Chambers. The schools and clubs that invited us in and gave us an opportunity to develop as coaches became part of who we are and what we bring to the field, and we are grateful to all of them. Our experience in Morgantown was not only incredibly fun, but also where we made our biggest strides as coaches. Thank you Nikki Goodenow and Nikki Izzo-Brown for all your help and support during our time there.

Our former and current players and their parents provided much of the inspiration for the stories and lessons that we share in this book. Players like Danny Swan and Kaitlin Parsons are why we coach and why we encourage others to get involved in this wonderful game. Thank you for your dedication to the sport.

We extend our sincere thanks to our friends at Human Kinetics: Justin Klug believed in us and helped convince us that we were ready for this challenge; Tom Heine was patient with us and offered ideas for improvement as well as deadlines; and Heather Healy spent many *long* hours synthesizing our ideas. We have enjoyed working with and learning from them.

Neil Bernstein was extraordinarily warm and professional throughout the photo shoot. He helped us organize the players and provided us with some laughter throughout the 30-degree day. We are very thankful to Chad Wallace and Sylvia Lane, who connected us with the administration and models from John Strange Elementary school. Kobe and his parents, Isaac and Nikki Webster; Taylor and her parents, Brian and Shelia Henry; Ethan and his mom, Amanda Dunn; Erika and her mom, Roberta Pioch; Jacob and his parents, Tony and Jennifer Dzwonar; Sophie and her parents, Kim and Steve Beck; and Jameson (our nephew) and his parents, Allison and Jason Blom; were all phenomenally cooperative. Despite being asked to wear short sleeves and shorts on a very cold, windy day, the players were patient, respectful, and eager to help us get the necessary pictures. Thank you to Mark Ellwein and Dynamo FC Soccer Club for the use of their facilities.

Key to Diagrams

Offensive player

Defensive player

Offensive player relocates here

Defensive player relocates here

Soccer ball

Offensive player starts with ball

Defensive player starts with ball

Goalkeeper

Goalkeeper starts with ball

Player

Player starts with ball

Coach

Cone

Cone used as goal

Path of player

Path of ball

Dribble

Help! Where Do I Start?

Within the last 20 years, most soccer organizations in the United States have embraced the idea of small-sided (or short-sided) soccer for children 12 and under. Children no longer play on a 120-by-80-yard (110 by 75 m) field, where they could barely run across the entire field without a break, touched the ball only two or three times a game, and rarely scored. The short-sided game allows players to get more touches on the ball, be more directly involved, and learn from the game, which all have increased their enjoyment of the sport. So what does this mean for you? You'll have only 6 to 10 players on your team instead of 15. Phew! Now managing 6 players doesn't seem that bad.

Children love this game because they get to run around outside and use their feet to play a sport. They enjoy playing because they get to be with their friends, eat orange slices at halftime, and drink juice boxes when it's all over. What more could a child ask for? Remember as you embark on this coaching journey that children learn to worry about winning from the adults in their lives; all kids really want is to run around and have fun. If you can keep this as your main focus throughout the season, you will do well—and you'll have fun too! Maintaining this philosophy will help when you are feeling frustrated or doubting yourself. We wish we could tell you that every day will be fabulous, but you know there will be challenges. We recommend always going back to the main question at hand: Are the children having fun? If the answer is yes, then relax and enjoy the chaos.

This chapter provides you with the information to get started. You can think of it as Coaching Youth Soccer 101, but you don't have to worry about a grade. In this section, you'll learn about equipment, the parts of the field, the basic positions, the rules you really need to know, and how to get the season started. Remember as you read the chapter that rules, field size, and markings vary by age group and league. We have provided you with standard information, but always refer to your league's guidelines and policies for the final word.

Coach's Equipment

The equipment you receive will vary from league to league. Unfortunately it will also vary in quality. Typically, coaches are provided with a few balls, a few cones, and an equipment bag. If you are lucky, you may receive a ball pump and some pinnies (pullovers) too. Whatever you are given, we will help you make do. Just remember that Pelé started his brilliant soccer career with a ball of rags, a dirt field, and no shoes. Look at what he was able to do!

The following list details the equipment you'll need in order to coach successfully:

- **Balls.** Soccer balls come in three main sizes (3, 4, and 5), and it is important to have the right size for your team. Players under the age of 8 use a size 3 ball. Players ages 9 to 12 use a size 4 ball, and players older than 12 use a full-size (size 5) ball. Balls can vary in quality, and you will quickly be able to tell the difference. If it feels like plastic or something you played kickball with in physical education, you should probably upgrade. Otherwise, if it is round and properly inflated, it will work. For beginners, especially, you want every player to have a ball, so using inexpensive balls is better than having a player without a ball.

- **Ball pump.** Be sure to have a pump and lots of extra needles at each practice and game. A pump is like an umbrella: If you have it with you, you probably won't need it; the day you forget it, all the balls will need air.

- **Cones.** Cones are typically shaped like a disc or a triangle. They are wonderful for setting up drills, small fields, makeshift goals, and obstacle courses. They can also serve as cone monsters, mines, goalkeepers, and mountains. If someone offers you cones, take them! Write your name on them in *permanent marker*, and keep an eye on them. Cones seem to disappear easily and reappear on someone else's field. Although cones are important to coaches, it's possible to go overboard. When you begin to have more cones on your field than players in the entire park, you may want to put a few away.

- **Whistle (or a loud voice).** You will also want a method of communication that can provide some structure to the organized chaos of the game. Because of the outside environment, you will need either a whistle or a loud voice so that your players can hear you. You need to get their attention before providing instructions, commands, praise, or encouragement; otherwise your efforts will go unheard.

- **Watch.** You will need a watch to time drills, count down the time to the end of practice, and know how close you are to the end of the quarter during games. Any watch will do, but a water-resistant stopwatch is best.

- **Coaching notebook.** This is a half-inch or one-inch binder that contains all your team's important information for the season. For example, you may want to include the game schedule and extra copies for the players who lose their schedules, a layout of the fields so you know where your game field is located, league rules, emergency contact sheets, player and parent contact information, and copies of practice plans from this book. You can also include any other documents that your league gives you or requires the players or parents to complete. (Some leagues will require parents or players to sign a code of conduct.)

- **Comfortable, weather-ready clothes.** Unfortunately, it always seems to be rainy, windy, or extra-hot at the soccer fields, no matter how nice it was when you left your house. You are welcome to coach in work clothes, but it will be a lot more fun if you wear comfortable, weather-ready clothes. We also recommend keeping a jacket with your soccer equipment so you will be prepared for a change in the weather.

- **First aid kit.** Band-Aids, ice packs, and kisses on boo-boos cure most problems, so we have found it helpful to have at least a small first aid kit. Your kit should include a variety of Band-Aid sizes, tape, gauze, instant ice packs, scissors, an antiseptic, tweezers, and sunscreen (remember that you are coaching an outdoor sport). If you are coaching children with long hair, you should also carry extra hair bands (or offer to use those scissors for discount haircuts).

- **Water.** Water is crucial not only for the players but for the coach as well. When you are feeling frustrated, you can use a water break as a time to recoup. So you will learn to really appreciate water. Even on cold days, make sure you have water for yourself and some extra for Forgetful Freddie who always leaves his water bottle at home. It is not safe to assume that the league practice facility will have a drinking fountain, at least not one close to the field.

- **Patience hat.** This imaginary cap may be your most important piece of equipment. Wearing your patience hat is a reminder that the goal is to have fun, that things don't have to be perfect and that you are volunteering your time to allow children to play a great game. Remember to put on this hat when players are fighting for your attention, when parents are critiquing your decisions, and when the league scheduler notifies you at the last minute of changes to Saturday's game. If your hat becomes misplaced at any time, distance yourself from others while you look for it.

If you are like most coaches, you won't always be leaving for the field from the same place. You might go straight from the office, school, church, or home. Remember to put the balls, cones, first aid kit, water, whistle, ball pump, and your jacket in the car before practices and games. If you can, we recommend just leaving the equipment in your car. It might stink a little, but some air freshener will fix that.

Kids' Equipment

Check with your league to confirm what equipment the players need. The league might be able to provide you with equipment for players who have limited funds. Ask your players to bring the following equipment to every practice and game:

- **Shin guards and socks.** Some kids love shin guards; others hate wearing the bulky plastic on their legs. Either way, they should always be mandatory, both at practices and at games. Shin guards provide the only real protection the kids have when other players are kicking at the moving target being dribbled down the field. Requiring them in practice helps keep the players safe and helps the players adjust to how they feel. Some shin guards have straps to go under the child's foot, while others do not. One type is not better than the other; it is just a matter of personal preference. All players should also wear socks that completely cover the shin guards to keep them in place as the players run up and down the field. Both pieces of equipment can be purchased at most sporting goods, department, or multipurpose stores for a fairly reasonable cost.

- **Appropriate shoes.** Although soccer cleats are recommended, they are typically not required in most leagues. Tennis shoes will work; they just do not provide much traction. Again, soccer cleats can be purchased at most sporting goods, department, or multi-purpose stores. Players should try on shoes while wearing a thick pair of socks (or their actual soccer socks) to ensure a proper fit. They should fit snugly on the foot but still allow for some growing room. Baseball and softball cleats are typically not legal for soccer.

- **Comfortable, weather-ready clothes.** Encourage your players to wear comfortable play clothes to practice. They should wear non-restrictive clothing that can get dirty. Even if there is only one small mud puddle in the entire complex, the players will find it, so play clothes are a must. The school uniform just won't cut it. For games, leagues will typically supply the jersey (usually a colored T-shirt) with the registration fee, but the parents may have to purchase shorts and sometimes the socks. Encourage the parents to throw an extra jacket and maybe a towel in the car to be prepared for the surprise evening shower or gusts of wind that hover over soccer fields.

- **Water bottle.** Encourage your players to bring a *full* water bottle with their name on it to all practices and games. Even if a parent plans to bring a sports drink or juice box, the players still need water.

- **Ball.** Because ideally you want a ball for every player (more balls than players would be even better), encourage all players to purchase and bring a ball with their name on it to practices. It is not as crucial for games, because you will need only a few balls for the warm-up.

Playing Field

If there is any grass on the field, then you are doing well. If there are lines on the field, you are doing very well! Don't expect a perfectly manicured putting green; rather, hope for a smooth, somewhat green surface. On the serious side, do take a stroll around the field before you begin practice or games just to make sure it is a safe surface, free of large rocks and divots. The league (or parks department) should be doing this, but it is a good practice to make it a habit.

The following explanations describe each marking that appears on a regulation soccer field (see figure 1.1). You probably won't see all these markings on your game field, especially with the younger age groups. The younger age groups play on smaller fields and play with

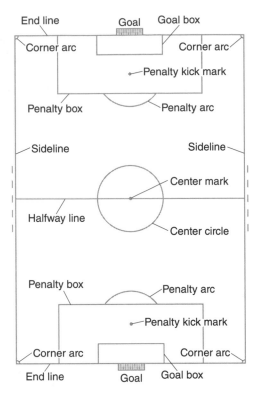

Figure 1.1   Proper markings for a regulation soccer field.

fewer rules, so fewer lines are needed in order to control the play of the game. Table 1.1 lists the lines you will typically see on the field for each age group. Please note that the lines will vary by leagues, so be ready to work with whatever lines are provided.

Table 1.1   Typical Field Markings by Age Group for Small-Sided Games

Age Group	End Lines	Sidelines	Halfway Line	Center Circle	Goal Box	Corner Arc	Penalty Box	Penalty Kick Mark	Penalty Box Arc
U6	✔	✔	✔	✔					
U8	✔	✔	✔	✔	✔	✔			
U10	✔	✔	✔	✔	✔	✔	✔	✔	✔
U12	✔	✔	✔	✔	✔	✔	✔	✔	✔

- **Center circle.** This circle appears in the middle of the field and is split by the halfway line. The radius of the circle varies from 6 to 10 yards (5 to 9 m), depending on the age group. Opposing players must be outside this circle during a kickoff.

- **Center mark.** This is the mark in the middle of the center circle to designate the kickoff spot.
- **Corner arc.** This arc is located at the intersection of the end line and sideline and has a 1-yard (1 m) radius. The ball must be placed inside this arc for a corner kick.
- **End lines (or goal lines).** These lines mark the ends of the field. The goals should be centered on this line. Spectators are not allowed to stand or sit behind the end lines.
- **Goals.** On a regulation field, the goal is 24 feet wide and 8 feet high. Although goal size varies by league, typically a U6 goal is 6 feet by 4 feet, a U8 is 12 feet by 6 feet, and U10 and U12 goals are either 18 feet by 6 feet or 21 feet by 7 feet.
- **Goal box (or goal area, or "the 6").** This small box in front of the goal is used to define the space in which the ball must be placed for a goal kick. For a regulation-size field, it is 6 yards (5 m) out from the end line.
- **Halfway line (or midline).** This is the line that divides the field into halves. Kickoffs are taken from the middle of this line at the center mark. This line defines whether a team is in its attacking or defending end of the field.
- **Penalty arc.** This is the half-circle at the top of the penalty box. The purpose of this mark is to ensure that all players are at least 10 yards (9 m) away from a player taking a penalty kick.
- **Penalty box (or penalty area, or "the 18").** This is the large box that extends out in front of the goal. Goalkeepers are allowed to use their hands anywhere inside this box. If a player (other than the goalkeeper) uses his hands or commits a hard foul (refer to the description of fouls in the "Rules of the Game" section later in this chapter) inside this box, the consequence is a penalty kick. For a regulation-size field, the penalty box extends 18 yards (16 m) out from the end line.
- **Penalty kick mark.** This is the mark on the field inside the penalty box from which a penalty kick is taken. On a regulation field it is 12 yards (11 m) from the end line; it is 8 to 10 yards (7 to 9 m) out on smaller fields.
- **Sidelines (or touch lines).** These are the lines on the long sides of the field. Typically players and coaches sit on one side of the field while parents and spectators are on the other side. Throw-ins are used when the ball goes over these lines.

League Rules

As the coach, you need to know all the league rules, which determine how games are managed. First you need to know how the soccer world in general and your league in particular determine a child's soccer age. Although some leagues use the calendar year to form age groups, most youth leagues use a cutoff date (usually around July 31) of the current year to establish the age groups. For example, if a player is 5 on July 31, then the player would be in the U6 age group, even if the player will turn 6 years old on August 2. The common age groups for youth soccer are U6, U8, U10, and U12.

In the younger age groups, teams are often coed, but it really depends on the size and philosophy of the league. If the league has a large group of participants, girls and boys may not play on the same team. However, if the league is small, there may be only a few teams, so everyone plays together or the teams are primarily made up of boys with a girl or two on each team. The philosophy of most recreation programs is to get as many children playing as possible, so the leagues are designed to maximize participation.

You'll need to be familiar with the various league rules. We've offered as much information as we can, but for some issues you'll need the specific rules for your particular league. You can get these answers from your league administrator when you attend the coaches' meeting before the season begins. Be sure you know the answers to the following questions:

- **How much practice time is allowed?** Even if your league allows for more, twice a week is the maximum you should practice. Now you may have a drill sergeant parent who wants the kids to do push-ups when they miss the goal, run laps when they are late, and practice every day, but two one-hour practices a week is plenty of soccer for recreational youth soccer players. If you have a U6 team, we recommend practicing only once per week when you start playing games. Less is more! It would be better for the kids to be hungry for more soccer time, not pouting because they "have to go" to soccer practice. Also, remind the players and parents that all soccer practice doesn't have to occur at practice. Encourage players who want more to spend time with the soccer ball in their yards or at a park near home. They can work on many of the same skills you show them at practice, and soccer can be played as a pickup game in the neighborhood as easily as any other sport.

- **What fields can we practice on?** It is important to know what field you will practice on so you can tell your players where to meet, especially if the complex is big and lots of teams practice at the same time. You may be able to always practice on the same field, but be ready to be flexible because of weather, other teams, and makeup games that may unexpectedly change your practice location. If the complex is smaller, then your issue will be related to finding and claiming space rather than finding your players. If 12 teams have to practice on three fields, space becomes a hot commodity. You don't need to camp out days in advance as if you are waiting for Duke basketball tickets. You do need to be prepared to share space with other teams and work in awkward spaces.

- **How many players can be on the field?** The number of players per team on the field depends on the age group (see table 1.2). The numbers may vary slightly by league and should directly relate to the number of players on your team. Typically leagues follow these guidelines:
  - U5 and U6 usually have 3 to 5 players on the field without goalkeepers.
  - U7 and U8 usually have 3 to 6 players on the field without goalkeepers.
  - U10 and U12 usually have 5 to 11 players on the field with goalkeepers.

- **Will goalkeepers be used?** Goalkeepers (keepers, goalies, GKs) are not typically used for U8 or younger (table 1.2), but you will want to confirm this at the beginning of the season. You don't want to get Sticky-Hands Stacey excited about playing in goal and then find out you need to find a place on the field for her.

Table 1.2 Regulation Summary by Age Group for Small-Sided Games

Age Group	Ball Size	Length of Game	Number of Players	Approximate Field Size
U6	3	5-8 min. quarters	3-5, no goalkeeper	20-30 yards (18-27 m) long × 15-25 yards (14-23 m) wide
U8	3	8-12 min. quarters	3-6, no goalkeeper	25-35 yards (23-32 m) long × 20-30 yards (18-27 m) wide
U10	4	20-25 min. halves	5-7, with goalkeeper	45-60 yards (41-55 m) long × 35-45 yards (32-41 m) wide
U12	4	25-30 min. halves	7-11, with goalkeeper	70-80 yards (64-73 m) long × 45-55 yards (41-50 m) wide

- **What are the playing time rules, and how do substitutions work?** Most recreational leagues mandate the number of quarters each player is required to play. The rule is usually at least two quarters per game per player. This is a very important rule to follow to ensure that each player gets a chance to participate. Because the quarters are short and you must keep track of playing time, typically substitutions are allowed only between periods (at quarter breaks and halftime). This may be frustrating at times when Shy Sammy is tired of playing and you still have 3 minutes left in the 5-minute quarter, but it helps to ensure that all players get their mandated playing time. Table 1.2 shows the length of periods commonly used for the various age groups.

- **How long are the games?** Again game length will vary by league and age group, ranging from 5-minute quarters to 30-minute halves. Typically there is not much time between quarters, just enough to substitute and have the players get a quick drink. You will not have time for your infamous pep talk, so be ready just to add a few words of encouragement and to remind them which goal they are to kick the ball into. Usually halftime is 5 to 10 minutes long.

- **Is anyone keeping score?** There is no universal rule about whether youth leagues require scores to be reported. The common practice is to not keep score until the U8 age group or maybe even U10. The idea is to decrease pressure and emphasize skill mastery over outcome, while protecting players' feelings, emphasizing good sporting behaviors, and preserving motivation. Unfortunately, even if your league does not keep score for your age group, some parents and players will keep score and will have the burning desire to share it with others. Quietly remind them that the focus of this age group is on participation and learning skills. You can be proactive by discussing this issue at the preseason parents' meeting. If the players (and even the parents) are set on counting something, give them something else to count. For example, ask them to keep track of the number of shots on goal, the number of saves made by the keeper, the number of times a player used the left foot, or the highest number of consecutive passes the team made. You can even change the "stat of the week" to mirror the themes from practice.

- **Who officiates the game?** The goal of small-sided recreational soccer is to allow the kids to play with as few interruptions as possible. Rules and officials disrupt the game and are really secondary when the score is not kept and safety is ensured. Typically, at the U6 level, coaches help maintain safety and direct the players when the ball goes out of bounds, so no official is needed. At the

U8 level, one official is usually assigned to a game, with the goal to keep the play going and stop play only for major infractions. Two or three officials are provided for U10 and U12 games. Remember to be nice to these officials. Being a referee is a tough job that lends itself to lots of criticism and very little appreciation. Furthermore, typical recreational youth soccer officials are inexperienced, volunteering, or young in age. Remember that all your players will be watching how you treat the officials, so you need to demonstrate positive ways of handling frustrating (or completely incorrect) calls. Your players will act according to the model you provide.

- **What are the rules for inclement weather?** It is very important to be ready for weather situations that can be unsafe. At the preseason coaches' meeting, be sure to ask what the league's procedures are for notifying coaches and parents when practices and games should be stopped or if the fields will be closed because of the weather. Some leagues post information on the league Web site, some have a weather hotline, and others rely on good judgment by the officials and coaches.

Rules of the Game

When coaching youth soccer, you don't need to get caught up in the specifics of every rule. If you can become familiar with the basics (which are presented in this section), then you will know enough to help the kids learn while they play. Since U5 and U6 games don't usually have referees, the only rules that are typically enforced are hand balls, blatant fouls, and out-of-bounds rules. If you aren't comfortable with all the rules of the game, this is a good age group for you to coach.

With each older age group, more rules are emphasized more strictly. If you would like to learn more about the official rules, check with your league or refer to the Web site of Fédération Internationale de Football Association (FIFA) at www.fifa.com. FIFA is the world soccer governing body that determines the official rules, but leagues often adjust the rules to suit the younger age groups.

Before you get excited and have a "rules" practice, remember that young players will forget all the rules once they start running around. They just want to play, and the goal of youth soccer is to let players have the freedom to play with minimal interruption. When explaining rules, keep it short and simple. Start with three basic rules: (1) Use your feet, not your hands, (2) stop when the whistle blows, and (3) kick the ball into the opposite goal.

Even though the first rule, *use your feet, not your hands*, seems simple, it is very unnatural. We spend hours every day using our hands, and we rarely use our feet, so the thought of playing a game for 20 to 60 minutes without using the hands is a stretch. Little Johnny will undoubtedly pick up the ball at some point, and when he realizes he was not supposed to do this, he will quickly drop the ball and look over at you for the next course of action. Just smile, tell him to keep playing, and move on.

The second rule, *stop when the whistle blows*, is helpful in maintaining some order on the field. Now we say *some* order because you obviously do not want the kids running all over the place, knocking people down to get the ball, or kicking the ball around out of the playing area, but recreational youth soccer is chaotic, and the small-sided game allows all the players to be involved and to learn from playing. Don't feel as if you need to have little soldiers on the field who are waiting for your next command. Let them figure things out. It is helpful to use a whistle so you can get the players' attention without yelling. Once you have their attention, then you can explain the rule violation.

The third rule, *kick the ball into the opposite goal*, will be broken almost as often as the first rule. No matter what you do, Meek Malinda will "score" her first goal by kicking the ball into the wrong goal. She will likely want to celebrate it just as if she had scored the winning goal in overtime, in the right end of the field. Celebrate with her, and then tell her next time to shoot it in the other goal. Most leagues do not require the score to be kept at the youngest age groups, so this is not a big deal. Even if the score is kept, stay focused on the number one reason that kids play soccer, which is to have fun, rather than the outcome of the game.

Kickoffs

Kickoffs are used to start a game or a new period and after a team scores. A coin toss can determine who will kick off in the first period, and then the teams alternate who kicks off next. For a kickoff, the ball is placed on the center mark, which is in the middle of the halfway line, inside the center circle. All players must be on their own half of the field at the start of the kickoff, and the team who is receiving the ball must be outside the center circle. The ball must be kicked onto the other team's half, and the kicker cannot touch the ball a second time until it is touched by someone else.

Out of Bounds

When the ball goes out of bounds, the ball is awarded to the team who did not send the ball out of bounds, and the ball is put back into play near the location where it went out of bounds. The way the ball is brought back into play depends on where the ball leaves the field. If the ball goes out of bounds on a sideline, it results in a throw-in. ("Yay, time to use our hands!") Unless you have a goalkeeper, this is the only time your players should use their hands. Be prepared to rotate who throws the ball in because your kids will be competing for the opportunity to use their hands. For a throw-in, the player stands outside the playing area close to where the ball crossed the sideline. The player must grasp the ball with both hands, bring it completely over the head, and release it onto the field of play. Both feet must stay on the ground during this time.

If the ball goes out of bounds on an end line, a goal kick or a corner kick is used to bring the ball back into play. If the ball goes over the end line by fault of the *attacking team* (the team trying to score), then the defending team puts it back in play through a goal kick. The ball is placed anywhere inside the goal box and must clear the penalty box with that initial kick. Most often the goalkeeper takes this kick because he is closest to the ball, but any player is allowed to take it. All other players, must stand outside the penalty box. If the ball goes out over the end line by fault of the *defending team* (the team protecting the goal), then the attacking team is awarded a corner kick. The attacking team inbounds the ball by kicking it from the corner arc. Players on the defending team must stand at least 5 or 10 yards (5 or 9 m) (depending on league rules) away from the corner arc during a corner kick.

Fouls

According to FIFA, a foul is a behavior that involves careless, reckless, or excessive force. Fouls are subjective by nature, so the best thing you can do is encourage your players to focus on the ball and keep their arms down by their sides. If they raise their arms to push off, then they are committing a foul. However, not all body contact constitutes a penalty. In youth recreational soccer, you will see kids fall, trip, kick, and bump into other players all the time. If a foul were called every time this happened, the kids would never get to play.

When a foul is called, it results in a free kick. At the site of the foul, the team who was fouled kicks the ball back into play. Depending on the league rules, the opposing team's players generally must stand at least 5 to 10 yards (5 to 9 m) away from the ball. The main purpose of foul infractions is to keep the play safe and fair. If safety is not an issue and the foul was not intentional, then let the player know the rule and let the play continue. If Out-of-Control Charlie doesn't slow down when he gets close to other players and continually knocks people down, you should talk to him and consider calling the fouls to help make the point. If Timid Tammy accidentally stumbles into Show-Off Sarah, just let it go.

Handling the Ball (Hand Ball)

Technically, handling the ball involves deliberately touching the ball with any part of the arm from the fingertips to the top of the shoulder. Now when a player is only 3 feet (90 cm) tall and the ball is the size of the entire arm, handling occurs often. Add this to the fact that it is abnormal to use our feet and not be able to use our hands, and you will get *lots* of handling. As a result, this rule is usually loosely enforced at the U6 and U8 levels, with a slightly stricter enforcement at the U10 level. At the U12 level, the rule is fully intact. Violation of the rule results in a free kick from the spot of the infraction. If it occurs inside the penalty box, a penalty kick is awarded.

Offside

The offside rule has given coaches, players, officials, and fans something to debate for years. A player becomes offside if she is past the second-to-last defender on the attacking side of the field and is in front of the ball (see figure 1.2). In other words, offensive players must either be behind the ball or have at least two opponents between them and the goal. The goalkeeper counts as one of the two opposing players. If a player runs behind the defender or goalkeeper while dribbling, there is no offside violation. If a player is even with the ball, the ball is passed behind the defenders, and she runs to get it, there is no offside violation.

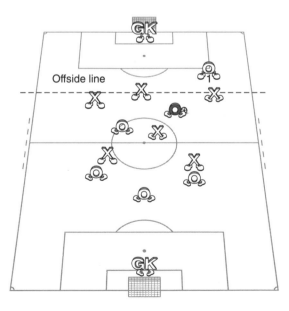

Figure 1.2 Because two defenders (including the goalkeeper) are not between player 1 and the goal, player 1 would be called offside if he or she received the ball in this position.

To complicate matters just a bit, a player who is in an offside position but isn't involved in the play is not considered to be in violation of the rule. For example, if Billy is running down the sideline offside, but the ball is passed to Jackson in the middle of the field, then it doesn't matter that Billy is offside. Also, if a player receives the ball directly from a goal kick, a throw-in, or a corner kick, then the player is not offside. The good news for some of you is that offside is not typically enforced in age divisions that don't use goalkeepers.

Goalkeeper Rules

Goalkeeper is a special position; it has a different set of rules (see chapter 7 for more information) and requires a different mind-set. The goalkeepers are the only players on the field who can legally use their hands, but only inside the penalty box. If the age group you're coaching is playing with goalkeepers, you'll need to know a few additional rules that pertain to this position:

- Goalkeepers must wear a distinguishable jersey from the other players and referees.
- Goalkeepers cannot use their hands if the ball was intentionally passed back to them by a teammate with the feet. (They can pick up the ball if the teammate used other legal parts of the body.)
- Goalkeepers have 6 seconds to put the ball in play after picking it up in the penalty box. They may pass, punt, drop-kick, throw, or dribble the ball back in play.
- Once the goalkeeper has control of the ball with one or both hands, other players may not kick the ball.

Player Positions

The positions used in soccer depend on the number of players on the field. However, some positions will always be predominantly responsible for attacking and some predominantly responsible for defending. Encourage all your players to get into the mind-set of both attacking and defending. Player movement should be fluid, and the goalkeeper is the only person who is contained to only one spot. Remember, positions are not static locations on the field; rather, they refer to player responsibilities. You will typically assign your players to the following four basic positions:

- **Defenders (or backs, fullbacks).** These players are the last line of defense, spending most of their time in the defensive third of the field. Their primary focus is on stopping the opposing team's scoring opportunities. Defenders can be further broken down into central and outside defenders.

- **Midfielders.** These players link the defense to the offense and have equal defending and attacking responsibilities. They utilize passing and ball control to help move the ball from the defensive third to the attacking third. Some midfielders play in the center of the field, while others play on the outside (wingers).
- **Strikers (or forwards).** These players focus on scoring. They are the team's main attacking force and spend most of their time in the offensive third.
- **Goalkeeper (or keeper).** This person is directly responsible for protecting the goal; the keeper is the only player allowed to use her hands in the penalty box.

Opening Meeting

After attending the coaches' meeting, it is official. You have been given your duties, handed your team, and provided with equipment. There is no turning back! Your next step is to contact your players and let them know about the first practice. At the first practice, it is helpful to have an opening meeting with the parents so everyone is on the same page at the start of the season. If you plan it well, you can convince everyone that you know what you're doing! We will give you a few tips on how to do this. You can even pass out the list of meeting topics if you really want to impress the parents.

At the beginning of the meeting, introduce yourself and ask the players and their families to do the same. Give a brief statement about how you will operate as a coach. You do not need to have a set philosophy; just let everyone know your thoughts on coaching and the purpose of the season. Then let the kids go play, and just talk with the parents. You will win over the kids because they don't have to sit through adult talk, and you can have the parents' undivided attention with fewer distractions. This is when you will get into the meat of the meeting. First discuss the equipment and the uniform needs. Let the parents know what the players should bring to practice as well as games.

Your next topic relates to safety. Ask the parents if there is any important medical information you should know about their children. For example, are there major allergies, asthma, learning disabilities, or past injuries? Let them know they can speak with you individually if they prefer, but emphasize the importance of knowing this information before there is an issue. Most leagues provide a medical form for parents to fill out. Make sure you obtain completed forms for each player on your team if they were not completed at registration. Also confirm that every parent or guardian has completed a liability waiver (this was probably done at registration, but just make sure).

Another important topic of discussion is the practice and game schedule. Let the parents know the time and day(s) of week the team will practice. Identify where you will practice as well so that you do not waste time searching for your players. If the game schedule has been posted, make copies of it to distribute to the parents. If it has not been finalized, let them know you will get the information to them when you receive it.

Next you should discuss the method of communicating information to all the parents. You may need to quickly contact everyone if the fields are closed because of inclement weather or if the time of a game changes. Undoubtedly, you will have situations that require quick group contact. Will you use a phone tree or e-mail? Whichever you decide to use, be sure to get correct contact information for everyone, and have the parents double- and triple-check it. Figure 1.3 provides a sample contact information form you can ask the parents to complete. You should also explain your preferred method of communication. How would you like parents to contact you, and what issues are appropriate for those discussions? Be clear with your communication expectations and preferences.

This is also a good time to talk about your plans if the weather gets bad during a practice or a game. Discuss where you will take the players for shelter if a storm comes, so the parents who aren't at the practice or game will know where to find their kids. If your practice and game locations will stay the same throughout the season, this will be easier than if the location changes each time. You'll also need to consider the particular weather dangers where you live to ensure that your plans are appropriate.

You'll want to find a solid shelter that is close enough to your practice field and that you and the kids can reach in a reasonable amount of time. If a shelter is not available, think about a plan to get the children into cars of parents who are watching practice until the other parents arrive. On days where the weather is questionable, you might also ask the parents to stick around the field. In the younger age groups, most of the parents typically stay during practices, but it won't hurt to make that request up front and again on those questionable days.

Also, take this time with the parents to let them know how they can help you this season. Do you need an assistant coach or an extra pair of hands at practice? Do you want someone to direct the phone tree? Other roles may include injury assistance provider, snack coordinator, team manager, postseason party planner, action photographer, or referee. Also ask if they have any other talents or resources to offer the team. Someone may surprise you with another way to make your job easier and the

Figure 1.3 Sample Information Card for Players

Player's Information

Player's name: _____ Nickname: _____

Age: _____ Date of birth: _____

Number of past seasons in soccer: _____

Current school: _____ Grade level: _____

Parents' or Guardians' Contact Information

Who is the main contact parent or guardian? _____

Mailing address: _____

E-mail: _____ Home phone: _____

Cell phone: _____

Circle preferred method of contact: e-mail / home phone / cell phone

Alternative contact: _____

E-mail: _____ Home phone: _____

Cell phone: _____

Circle preferred method of contact: e-mail / home phone / cell phone

Who will typically be transporting the player to practice?

_____

Additional Information

Please specify any health concerns that the coaches should be aware of during practices and games (allergies, injuries, psychological issues, physical disabilities, and so on). _____

_____

Please list any specific equipment that your child should wear during practices or games (sport eye glasses, knee brace, ankle wrap, and so on).

_____

Please describe any information that will assist the coaches in helping your child have a favorable soccer experience. _____

From L. Blom and T. Blom, 2009, *Survival Guide for Coaching Youth Soccer* (Champaign, IL: Human Kinetics).

experience more fun for the players. Ask parents complete a volunteer assistance form (see figure 1.4) so you'll know which responsibilities you can delegate to parents.

You definitely want to have the parents sign up to bring snacks and drinks for after the games. Many children attend the games in anticipation of the halftime or postgame snacks. How simple life is! It is best to assign snack duty for the entire season as soon as you receive your game schedule. You will have many disappointed children if they do not get their juice boxes, so be sure to ask parents to switch dates with another parent if they cannot attend the game on their scheduled day. Be sure to give the parents some snack ideas. For halftime snacks, orange slices or quartered bananas are best to accompany water. You do not want your players to eat too much before they run back out onto the field. After the game, the sky is the limit. Sports drinks or juice boxes are great along with fruit snacks, muffins, or snack packs of cookies or crackers. This is really one of the most important steps to ensuring a successful season. A hungry kid is usually not a happy kid.

End the meeting with a brief recap and a few tips on how everyone can work together to create a positive experience for the kids. This is a

---

Figure 1.4   Volunteer Assistance Form

Circle the responsibilities you are willing to help with during the season.

Assistant coach   Practice helper   Team manager

Phone tree coordinator   Postseason party planner   Snack coordinator

Referee   Action photographer   Parent sideline manager

Injury assistance provider   Equipment manager

Please list any other talents or resources you would like to offer the team:

_____

_____

_____

From L. Blom and T. Blom, 2009, *Survival Guide for Coaching Youth Soccer* (Champaign, IL: Human Kinetics).

good time to state a few expectations about parent sideline behavior. Express how important it is for parents to be supportive of all the children playing in the game, even the opponents. Let them know that the most helpful comments from the sideline are cheering and encouraging words. (See chapter 11 for more information on working with parents.) You can also give the parents some helpful tips about communicating with their children after the games. We like to end our opening meetings with the things parents should say to their kids after each game:

- I love you.
- I love to watch you play.
- Did you have fun?
- What can I get you to eat?

If parents can stick to these four things, the kids will be happy and motivated to attend the next practice or game. If the kids are happy, the coach is probably very happy.

The Coach's Clipboard

✔ If the kids are having fun, even if they are not doing everything exactly right, then you are doing well!

✔ Since Band-Aids and ice packs dry most tears, be sure to have some with you.

✔ At all practices and games, require players to wear shin guards and socks that cover the guards.

✔ Encourage your players to purchase a ball and bring it to every practice.

✔ Know the league rules (number of players on the field, length of games, and playing time and substitution rules).

✔ When explaining the rules to your players, start with (1) no hands, (2) stop when you hear the whistle, and (3) kick the ball into the opposite goal.

✔ Encourage players to be involved in defending and attacking.

✔ Remember that positions are defined by responsibilities, not restricted to parts of the field.

✔ Meet with the parents at the start of the first practice to go over important information.

Organizing Your Team Practices

Typically new coaches are nervous about practice time because they actually have to do some coaching. Games are easy because you can just let the kids play, but during practices you are supposed to teach them something, and how can you teach them something you don't know? Well, that is where this book can help. You don't have to make the kids soccer experts this season; you just want to provide a safe and fun environment where they can learn. This chapter will help you learn how to plan practices that are effective, efficient, and fun. All right, Coach. It's time to design the master plan, so let the strategery begin. Remember, patience and persistence will get you through it!

Designing a Practice

Before you can unload your inner Lombardi on these future all-stars, you've got a few choices to make. When designing a practice you must first decide the purpose, or theme, of the session. This may seem odd at first. After all, the purpose is for the players to get better, right? Yes, that's always the goal, but, more specifically, the theme of the practice might be to improve a particular weakness, introduce a concept, or just have some good old-fashioned fun. It is up to you to decide what the focus of each practice will be. The factors that influence this decision may be the time frame within the season, an evaluation of previous performance, an upcoming competition, or the current mental and physical state of your players. Some examples of practice themes include shooting, crossing, passing, receiving, dribbling, and defending.

Early in the season, you'll typically introduce new skills and topics. Later on, as you think the players have begun to master some of the basics, you can challenge them with something new. After the team has played a game or two, you can cater your practices toward a specific weakness you observed during the game. In this case, help the players build from whatever they did well (there must be something). On occasion, you may discover that you and the kids just need a break. This is a good opportunity to get the parents involved in a scrimmage or to run a few of the drills you know the kids really like.

As you choose a specific theme, try to be realistic about how much information your players can handle. Choose two to four key points that you want to make, and choose activities that reinforce these points. For example, if you choose passing as your practice theme, then you may choose to emphasize (1) using the inside of the foot, (2) pointing the plant foot toward the target, and (3) following through after kicking the ball. Your practices will be most meaningful if players repeatedly hear the same few points. When their parents ask them what they learned, they'll be able to repeat your points. If players want to work on something before the next practice, they'll be able to easily recall the main concepts you covered.

Although your planning, coaching, and emphasis for practice are narrow and specific, your team's experience at practice will include a wide range of positive aspects. It's like a school field trip. There is a set destination that is related to the school curriculum, but the experiences the kids have encompass more than the academic objectives. Players at your practice are learning a lot about the game and becoming more aware of many of their own abilities, even when you have a specific set of coaching points for a given session. Most important, you should always work to see that they are having fun.

Five Parts of a Practice

Now that you have a practice theme, you should spend some time organizing drills and activities that focus on that theme. This is your lesson plan for the day. The first thing you want to consider is your overall practice time. For recreational soccer teams, 45 to 60 minutes of actual practice time on the field is plenty, but factor in a few extra minutes for water breaks, transitions, and any discussions you might need to have with the players or the parents. And unless you plan on picking up all your players on the way to the field, you can expect one or two kids to be late. Your local league may dictate how much time you actually have if field space is an issue for the number of teams in your organization.

Plan the progression of your practice to include five parts: skill warm-up, skill training, team training, games, and cool-down. Five parts may seem like a lot, but those parts often overlap, and the cool-down for this age group is minimal. Use the practice template provided in figure 2.1 to plan your weekly sessions. With a little planning, a good skill warm-up

Figure 2.1 Practice Planning Template

Coach: _____   Date: _____

Time: _____

Age Group: _____ Theme: _____

Practice part	Duration	Equipment	Activity or drill
Skill warm-up	5-10 min.		
Skill training	10-15 min.		
Water break			
Team training	10-15 min.		
Water break			
Games	10-15 min.		
Cool-down	5 min.		

From L. Blom and T. Blom, 2009, *Survival Guide for Coaching Youth Soccer* (Champaign, IL: Human Kinetics).

will take care of getting the kids ready to play and allow them to start working on the day's topic. Water breaks should be taken after the skill training and after the team training. Each break should be about 1 to 3 minutes. These breaks provide time for the kids to rest or to goof around and not have to follow directions, and they give you time to set up the next drill.

For the drills in chapters 3 through 8, we've identified which practice parts the drills are appropriate for. In addition to skill warm-ups, you'll need some pregame warm-ups. These warm-up drills are designed to allow your players to practice a variety of skills within a single drill so you can use your pregame time efficiently. The focus for a pregame warm-up is all-inclusive, while the focus for practice warm-ups is skill specific. You'll also need some drills to use when you want to let the kids have some fun competition. These can be used at the end of practice when you have extra time, when you want to reward the players for a good practice, or when you and the players just need a change of pace.

Skill Warm-Up
Warming up for 5 to 10 minutes is an important part of getting your practice started. For young players, the mental aspect of warming up is as important as the physical benefits. Design the warm-up around the theme of the practice, so the players are thinking about soccer and what they are going to learn. The intensity level should be fairly low at the beginning of the warm-up and then should slowly increase.

Start the warm-up with one or two activities the kids are familiar with or that require little actual instruction. The players need a couple of minutes to transition from their other activities and the car ride before they will be ready to learn something new and challenging. Dribbling a ball, making short passes, or simply jogging around in an area while changing direction and speed are easy ways to get the kids moving and encourage them to start getting focused. Choose activities that will get their heart rates up.

After the activities, lead the players through a brief, light stretch. Stretching cold muscles is like pulling on gum that hasn't been chewed yet, which is why you want to get their bodies warm first. To avoid injuries, the U.S. Youth Soccer Association recommends having players break a sweat (by speeding up their heart rates) before stretching.* For younger age groups, do not spend too much time on stretching; the kids' muscles are still pretty flexible, but taking a few minutes to stretch does help to establish good warm-up routines for the future. (See pages 214-216 in chapter 10 for warm-up activities and stretches.)

*www.usyouthsoccer.org

Skill Training   The skill training part of your practice is where the players get most of their touches on the ball. Typically, this part of a practice should last 5 to 15 minutes; however, for younger teams, this part of practice may frequently be the longest and may include several drills. You should have a ball for each player or every two players. Skill training should include drills that teach specific skills, with close attention paid to the players' technique.

Team Training   Team training refers to the transition stage in practice where the technical skills are put into play in gamelike drills and situations. For these 10 to 15 minutes, maintain a strong emphasis on proper technique, and reiterate the coaching points introduced during the warm-up and skill training. At the same time, incorporate playing against a defender, working in a specific direction, utilizing the help of teammates, or some other gamelike condition. A ball for every two to four players is appropriate for young players; a ball for every three to six players is appropriate for older kids.

Games   In this part of the practice, players are put in true game situations, typically with teams playing against one another and two goals incorporated into the drills. For these 10 to 15 minutes, place fewer restrictions on the players than in the team training session, but still encourage them to focus on the topic of the day. A big component of this part of your practice is making players more aware of the entire field, along with their teammates and opponents, as well as teaching them how to transition from offense to defense and vice versa. Chapters 5 and 6 provide appropriate drills for this part of the practice. You can also use scrimmages that emphasize the practice theme.

Cool-Down   A good cool-down is crucial for older, more competitive athletes, but still relevant for younger players. The main purposes are to allow the players to warm down and remind them of the key coaching points from practice, congratulate them on a good practice, and possibly assign a take-home challenge (see Making Practice Last All Week, page 32). Your cool-down can be 5 to 10 minutes or just a couple of minutes if you're running short on time. Design it so the kids are slowing down their pace. You do not need to include a specific drill; rather have the players complete light movement activities, like jogging, walking backwards, skipping, etc. Feel free to be creative. You can include the balls, relate the activity to the theme of the day, or just have the kids jog around to collect the cones and other equipment.

Finish the cool-down by stretching. You can use the same stretches that you used in the warm-up. As with stretching in the warm-up, if you include stretching now, the kids will understand as they get older that it's a regular part of practice. Stretching at the end of an intense workout and after cool-down can improve flexibility and muscle recovery. As you wrap up the stretching, give the players some specific feedback on the day's accomplishments. If you have any important announcements about schedules, fees, or upcoming events, put them in writing or at least make sure the parents are within earshot.

Hey, Coach, Can We Scrimmage?

Scrimmaging sometimes gets a bad rap, but a little gamelike practice can be exactly what young players need. It's the best way for them to get a feel for what a game will be like. The key to making scrimmages productive is to conduct a controlled scrimmage in which you take a more active role in helping players learn from the game. In this situation, you may restrict how many times players can touch the ball before they have to pass it or award extra points to a team for successfully demonstrating the practice theme in a game situation. You can also stop the scrimmage occasionally to point out something positive that has happened, such as a great pass or good positioning on the field, to reinforce intelligent play and ideal behaviors. Simply ending each practice with a scrimmage is probably not the best use of time, but a controlled scrimmage can be very effective and fit well in the games part of practice.

Making the Most of Practice

The concept of a five-part practice is meant to simplify your job as a coach and help make your practices effective and meaningful. By focusing your activities around a few specific and related coaching points, you more easily keep the players' attention and reinforce their progress. Here are a few tips that can help you make the most of each practice:

- **Keep them moving.** Avoid having players stand in long lines; use circles instead.

- **Keep a ball at their feet as much as you can.** Players become more comfortable with using their feet only if they have lots of opportunity to touch the ball.

- **Change activities every 5 to 7 minutes.** The guideline for attention span is about 2 to 5 minutes per year of age (20 minutes maximum). This may seem like a lot of change, but it doesn't have to be a completely new activity, just an adjustment or a variation to the instructions.

- **Change pace.** Because children have limited aerobic capacity, mix in walking, jogging, running, and sprinting so they will stay fresh longer. This is also more gamelike than constant jogging.

- **Keep instruction simple and short.** Be careful not to overcoach. In fact, you should err on the side of undercoaching. If you give players too much to think about, they will just become overwhelmed and frustrated. Try to demonstrate what you want them to do whenever possible (or have a player demonstrate). You can also ask a player's big brother or sister to demonstrate a skill. If players can hear the directions and watch what to do, they will be more likely to keep up.

- **Create opportunities to be successful.** Balance challenges with reality. When the kids feel successful, they will be motivated to take on new challenges. As Tony DiCicco, former coach of the U.S. women's soccer team, writes, you should catch them being good. Stopping play to point out something positive leaves a longer impression than criticizing and punishing. Kids want to please the important adults in their lives.

- **Use logical consequences for behavioral problems.** Logical consequences are outcomes to misbehaviors that relate to what would naturally happen if the child's behavior were allowed to continue. For instance, if a player is not listening and interferes with a drill, then he does not get to participate in the drill. He can sit out until he is ready to listen. Punishments such as making players do extra running don't actually teach the proper behavior. Besides, running is a good thing, and it is important for more advanced players. If it is used as a punishment, children may associate it as a negative action.

- **Let them play!** Soccer is a players' game; that is what draws kids to the sport. Let them play, and let the game be the teacher.

Expecting the Unexpected

One of the challenges of recreational sports is the unorganized nature of the beast. Most of the people involved are volunteers, just like you, and although they may have soccer experience, they may lack strong organizational skills and certainly lack time. Couple that with an uncontrollable outdoor playing environment, and it would be a surprise if you didn't encounter a few unexpected challenges. We can't predict every issue that might arise, but here are some common issues that, without a little coaching creativity, could interrupt your perfect plans.

For most leagues, field space is limited. Every coach wants a space of her own on the best field, close to the bathrooms, with lights and two goals every Tuesday and Thursday. Unfortunately, there are not enough perfect practice areas (if your league has any of those) for everyone, and the younger the age group, the lower the chance that an ideal space will be available.

So, you can camp out the night before or send your meanest, scariest parent out to reserve your field, or you can stay in your bed and be the coach of the year by being creative with the space that is available to you (although it won't hurt to have a parent keep an eye out during practice to see if a field opens up). Hopefully you will have some field space sometimes, but on the other days, use your cones (or parents—they make great goalposts!) to mark a practice space, and get to work. The kids will follow your lead; if you don't make it a big deal, they certainly won't care.

Another challenge is that you won't have every player at every practice. Of course, on the day you have the perfect practice planned or intend to practice the most important skill for your team's success, only a few kids will show up, and they will probably be the most skill-challenged players on your roster. One option is to pout and scream, making the kids who did show up miserable, but a better approach is to be flexible. Remember you're coaching youth soccer, not preparing for the World Cup. Besides, you don't have to throw away all your hard work. Take one of the following approaches instead:

- Put your plan aside until the next practice. Pull out this book and pick a more individualized skill to focus on, or use one of the practice plans (see chapters 3 through 7).
- Ask another coach (of the same age group) if he wants to practice together.
- Ask the parents to join the practice and serve as practice partners. (The parents probably need to learn more than the kids do.)
- Let the kids pick their favorite games, and have a fun day.

Use whatever choice makes sense for the situation, and enjoy the change of pace.

Managing the Personalities of Your Players

You will have some very interesting stories at the end of this season, and many of them will involve encounters with your players. We cannot cover all the unique personalities that may be a part of your team, but we can give you tips for dealing with some common player personalities that require a unique approach. In general, remember to have fun, and try to enjoy the differences among the children. Avoid the tendency to make a kid run or do push-ups for not fitting the typical player model. This may work in the military, but it is not a great solution for youth soccer. Besides, your practice sessions would be boring if all the children were exactly the same!

Shy Sammy   Sammy probably does not want to participate in some of the drills or interact much with the other players. No problem; just let him work things out at his own pace. There is no need to force him to participate or make him run laps for not following directions. Ask Sammy and his parents what would help him feel more comfortable. Sammy may not be able to identify anything that will help, and if he cannot, allow him to sit on the side (where you can see him), and tell him to join you when he is ready. Sammy probably needs to feel out the situation before playing. Meet his needs, and put your time into the players who are ready to play.

Chatty Cathy   Cathy has something to say all the time. You won't get her to be quiet in your short time together, so channel her energy in another fashion. It is important to get players to communicate on the field. See if you can get her to communicate, productively, to her teammates. For example, she can tell them, "Good job," or give instructions about who to pass to or when to shoot. Respect her energy; find ways to use it to the team's advantage.

Wimpy Wally   Wally wants to play soccer! He can't wait for practice. He has his socks and shin guards on at 4:00 even though soccer doesn't start until 5:30, but when it comes time to actually run around on the field and risk falling down, getting dirty, or bumping into someone, he is not interested. Wally is not ready to risk hurting himself, so he will not put himself in that situation. This is a challenging player to coach in a game that involves contact. Let him participate on his own terms, and avoid drawing attention to his wimpy outbreaks. Instead, cheer and praise him when he does take a risk—any risk. If he fails, tell him, "Good work!" for trying the activity. When he plays hard, give him a high five . . . but not too hard!

Helpful Henry

If there were a pitcher's helper in soccer, it would be Henry. He wants to be right by your side, assisting you with everything you do. You could shoo him away as if he were a sand gnat buzzing around your ear, or you could think, *Perfect. I need an assistant coach to help with the little things*, and allow him to help you. He can pick up the balls, lay down cones, fill the cups, or get the pinnies when you need more. Keep him busy, and he will be a happy camper.

Misfit Maggie

Poor Maggie doesn't seem to fit in on your team. She probably feels like this in most situations. It may be because she acts differently or even looks different from the other kids on your team. Regardless of her soccer skills, work to include her, and model the way the kids should treat her. If you have a player who is nice to everyone, ask this player to befriend her. Peer pressure can work negatively and positively, so this time, use it to your advantage. This is also a good argument for not letting players pick their partners during partner activities. You can avoid isolating Maggie by rotating partners and placing her with teammates who will accept her. Also, focus on what she does bring to the team instead of what she lacks. When she does something helpful or good, be sure to point it out to the team so they begin to appreciate her.

Out-of-Shape Oscar

Unfortunately, many kids do not get regular physical activity, and their fitness levels are poor. It would be easy to put Oscar on the sideline or make him run laps by himself, but neither will help him progress athletically. Ideally, you want to help him improve his fitness level and feel good about physical activity. His next coach will thank you. Avoid highlighting his weaknesses, and focus on his strengths. Does he want to be the goalkeeper? Can he take the goal kicks because of his strength? Even if Oscar is just a nice kid, that is still a plus. Allow him to participate as he feels comfortable, but also get him to push himself a little more each practice. You can even set goals with him. For example, at the beginning of the season he may be able to play for only 10 minutes without needing a break. Challenge him to increase that time to 15 minutes in two weeks. Set a goal that you know he can achieve, so that when he does he'll be motivated to keep improving.

Tattletale Tina

Tina is the team police officer. She is going to keep track of all the misbehaviors of her team members. You will have to address this behavior early in the season. Tell her that you appreciate her feedback, but you want her to tell you about the other players' behavior only when someone might get hurt. Another approach is to inform her that she can tell you about someone else's behavior only twice at each practice, and once the two times are up, she cannot tell you about any more situations. Hopefully she will then want to use her two times wisely, so she will spend her time processing whether she will tell you. If she persists in reporting to you, ask her to tell you about the good things that happen.

Keep in mind that nicknames are a fun way for kids to feel special. The general rule is to catch them being good, thereby reinforcing when they do things well, rather than spend your time telling them to behave or punishing them. You won't win many points with the kids or their parents if you actually call Terry "Temper Tantrum Terry." So if you assign a goofy nickname to a challenging personality, just make sure to use good judgment when you decide whether it is a nickname to use with the kids or just one to laugh about on your own to keep you sane.

Making Practice Last All Week

Because you will spend only one to three hours a week working with your players, they will need ways to improve outside of your direct teaching time. So hand out your business card at the team meeting, explaining that you charge $100 an hour for individual instruction! If that doesn't work, give them something they can do on their own, with a friend, or with their parents. You do want the players to practice their skills at times when they are not with you, and you want their parents to help teach them the correct techniques.

One of the best ways to get players of all ages motivated to put in quality practice on their own time is to give them work to do at home. In other words, give them homework just like they get at school. Just be smarter than the teachers; call it a *take-home challenge*, and leave out the word *work*. Take-home challenges should be specific goals that relate to the skills you covered that week at practice and can be accomplished in the given time at home. Here are some examples of challenges you can give:

- "Your challenge between now and Thursday's practice is to touch the ball 100 times with both feet." (Leave it open on how they touch the ball because you just want them to begin to get comfortable with those feet.)

- "This week your challenge is to learn or invent a new dribbling move that you can show the team at next week's practice."
- "The challenge for this week is to practice dribbling on the run from your dog, your brother or sister, or your parent. Have your opponent chase you 10 times while trying to get the ball."

The challenge should be something that every player could accomplish if he tried. It should also be stated in clear, specific, measurable terms. Kids like concrete directions. Give them reasonable numbers. You can even add to the challenge by saying, "If you reach the goal, then do it again."

Another way for players to improve their skills away from team practice is to teach their parents how to help them. Although you may have a few parents with soccer experience, many of them will be less comfortable with the game than you are. If you don't want the players using their hands or learning how to "block out" or "boot it" (common parental phrases), you will want to coach the parents, too. You can do this by allowing the parents to listen when you give coaching points, occasionally including parents in practice time, or suggesting that all parents buy this book. Whatever your method of choice, be sure to communicate at least basic skill information to the parents.

The Coach's Clipboard

✔ Identify the purpose of the practice: to improve a weakness, learn a new skill or concept, or have fun.

✔ Select one main theme for each training session.

✔ Emphasize two to four coaching points throughout the entire practice.

✔ Remember the five parts of an effective practice: (1) skill warm-up, (2) skill training, (3) team training, (4) games, and (5) cool-down.

✔ Water breaks allow the kids to take a break from focusing and allow you to set up the next activity.

✔ Scrimmage with a purpose; emphasize the theme of the day rather than allowing a free-for-all game.

✔ If players misbehave, use logical consequences (such as sitting out) rather than physical activity (such as running or push-ups) when reprimanding.

✔ Be prepared with a creative alternative on days when attendance is low or you don't get the best playing space.

✔ Appreciate and do your best to work with the wide array of personalities of the players on your team.

✔ Make practice last all week by assigning take-home challenges.

Teaching Dribbling Skills With 10 Simple Drills

Swarm ball, herd soccer, mass chaos—whatever you want to call it—is the typical formation seen on youth soccer fields all over the country. You'll see kids converging on the ball as if it were a pinata filled with their favorite candy. It doesn't seem fair that there is just one soccer ball out there for 6, 8, 12, and eventually 22 kids. It won't take long to realize that one of the keys to successful soccer is finding open space on the field. When you are coaching youngsters, the space is the 85 percent of the field that no one is standing on—essentially everything outside of a 10-yard (9 m) radius of the ball. Now, getting players to see the space can be difficult, and having them actually move into the space, well, that will wake you up with cold sweats in the middle of the night.

To help you sleep comfortably through the night, you will want to teach your players how to dribble the ball. That is really the essential starting point for your players. Dribbling is simply the act of moving the soccer ball down the field with one's feet. When there is open space in front of them, players will dribble faster and the ball may not stay close to them. When they are in traffic, players will need to be in better control of the ball so as not to lose possession. They will also need to be prepared to slow down, speed up, move to the side, or turn around. Being comfortable dribbling a soccer ball takes a great deal of practice. The good news is that the players will get that practice during every training session, every

No Soccer in the House, But . . .

One way to really help players learn to use their feet is to give each player a tennis ball or a small stuffed soccer ball to keep at home. Encourage them to roll the ball around with their feet when they are watching television or moving from room to room. You don't want to be blamed for their breaking furniture or knocking down lamps, so remind them to be careful and roll it only on the floor.

Encourage the players to use their feet to move the soccer ball all the time. Instead of carrying the ball across the field before or after practice, they should dribble it with their feet. When helping you gather the equipment or when shagging balls, they should use their feet. (Plan for the equipment gathering to take a little longer as a result.) As using their feet begins to feel more natural, you will have an easier time helping them learn to turn, change directions, start, stop, and, before long, even do some of the moves included in this chapter.

game, and almost every drill. Remember, patience and persistence will get you through the first dribbling practices.

Initially, the key point you should focus on for dribbling is simple: feet, not hands. The natural instinct for most of your kids will be to reach down and stop the ball with their hands. If they are trying to turn around and go the other way or move the ball around a cone, they will want to use their hands. Explain to them from the beginning that soccer players use their feet. Be prepared to say, "Feet, feet!"—a lot.

Designing a Dribbling Practice

One of the greatest aspects of young children is their determination to succeed at a simple task. They are likewise motivated by that feeling of success and excited to recapture that same feeling of accomplishment over and over again. This is important to remember. You should design most of your early practices and drills so that the kids can be successful. For dribbling, this means setting up three conditions to help them succeed: Allow the kids to initially practice in slow motion, without defenders, and with lots of space.

When you teach a new dribbling move, encourage the players to move like a turtle, in slow motion. Then as they become more comfortable with the move, encourage them to move faster, moving up to game speed, like a cheetah. Early on the drills should not include defenders. If players are under too much pressure before successfully learning a skill, they will use any method to be successful, and this often leads to practicing with poor technique. Provide open space and lots of it! If players are dribbling side by side across an area, make sure there is plenty of room between them. If they are dribbling inside a grid, make the grid large enough so the players can easily avoid running into one another. There is a time for creating traffic and challenging the players to dribble in a confined space, but this should come after the players have had time to familiarize themselves with dribbling the ball.

When putting together a dribbling practice, remember the five parts of a practice from chapter 2. If you are going to focus on dribbling during a practice, you want to focus on it for the *entire* session. By staying focused on just one theme during practice, you avoid overloading your players with instruction and feedback about a variety of topics. This chapter provides 10 basic drills, but you should use only three to five of the drills within a single practice. Keep the kids moving by changing activities, but do not become a drill sergeant. Figure 3.1 provides a sample dribbling practice.

In this chapter, we present 11 examples of footwork skills and dribbling moves for your players. If you are coaching really young players or beginners, focus on the footwork skills. The dribbling moves are for older players and those who are already fairly comfortable with dribbling.

There are certainly lots more moves out there, but if players can focus on and master just a few moves, they will be able to use them successfully in game situations, and their excitement and confidence with the ball will grow. If players have too many moves to learn, they will likely not master any of them, and then their confidence when taking on an opponent will be diminished. It is better for them to become skilled at one or two moves than to have a pocketful of moves they cannot use effectively.

If you have players who are excited about learning and want to work independently outside of practice, they can find other moves in books or on the Internet, or they could watch older players. Reinforce their enthusiasm, but try to be realistic about the amount of information you give your young players during any practice. Be aware of the progress your players are making, and try to balance challenging them with helping them be successful.

Developing Basic Footwork Skills

As the players become more comfortable with the concept of using just their feet, you should begin to challenge them to use all the different surfaces of both their right and left feet. By surfaces, we mean the

Figure 3.1 Sample Dribbling Practice Plan

Coach: _____ Date: _____

Time: _____

Age group: <u>Any</u>   Theme: <u>Dribbling</u>

Practice part	Duration	Equipment	Activity or drill
Skill warm-up	10 min.	1 ball for every player; cones to create boundaries in playing area	*Traffic cop* (see page 54) *Knockout* (see page 57) *Stretching*
Skill training	5-10 min.	1 ball for every player; 1 cone for every 2 players	*Mirror mirror* (see page 58)
Water break			
Team training	10-15 min.	1 ball for every 2 players; 12-20 cones to create gates	*Gates* (see page 61) This could lead well into a 1v1 drill where players are competing in a small space trying to score on the opponent.
Water break			
Games	10-15 min.	1 ball (plus a few extras off to the side), 2 goals (cones for goals), and pinnies	*Individual attacking scrimmage* (see page 62)
Cool-down	5-10 min.	Balls that were used during practice	*Ball collection:* On your command, players run to a ball, then dribble toward the parents who are watching. They must demonstrate two moves to the parents and then dribble to you. This can be repeated until all the balls have been collected. *Stretch* when finished.

From L. Blom and T. Blom, 2009, *Survival Guide for Coaching Youth Soccer* (Champaign, IL: Human Kinetics).

top, bottom, inside, and outside of each foot. The only thing they really shouldn't use is their toes. Although this may be the easiest way for many of the kids to push the ball forward early on, using the toes is an extremely difficult habit to break (and can really hurt!). Instead, encourage them to point their toes down toward the ground and push the ball with their shoelaces (see figure 3.2). This is the technique they will eventually use when they are able to run at speed while dribbling the ball in space. For now, show them where the toes go and what parts of the foot should be hitting the ball.

Figure 3.2   Dribbling with the laces.

When players are dribbling in a confined space or when there are other players close by (which is pretty much all the time at this age), encourage them to use the inside of their feet for most of the touches on the ball. The inside of the foot is the largest surface for them to use, so controlling the ball and the direction it is headed should be easiest using this technique. Also, this provides the most natural movement for controlling how firmly or softly the player is pushing the ball forward. When showing players how to use the inside of the foot, have them focus on kicking the ball with the middle of the inside of their cleats. You can point out that their shoes may have logos in this spot, which can give them a visual cue to use. As they begin to attempt turning with the ball or changing directions of their dribble, using the inside of the foot is typically the first method they will master.

During your drills, demonstrations, and activities, also encourage the players to use the outside of their feet to move and change directions with the ball as well as the bottoms of their feet. During games, the ball will roll around and end up on all different sides of the players, and the space they ultimately want to get into with the ball may be anywhere. The more comfortable the players are with using all the surfaces of both feet, the more successful they will be in game situations. You can challenge players to use both feet and different parts of each foot by placing certain restrictions on them in drills and practice situations.

There are a number of ways players can become more comfortable and confident with the ball at their feet. The four fast footwork skills that follow should be introduced individually but could be used together in practice once the players understand them. For each one, players should be light on their feet so they can quickly shift their weight, maintain balance, and move the ball crisply. All these activities make excellent take-home challenges. As with all skills, have players start very slowly, like a turtle, practicing the skill in a walking mode. As they feel more comfortable with the movement, they can speed up and move quickly, like a puppy, and then very quickly, like a cheetah, to reach gamelike speed.

Step-Ups   Step-ups are a little like walking up stairs. Players stand directly behind the ball and step, one foot at a time, up onto the ball. The movement will look similar to running in place as the players tap the balls of their feet onto the top of the ball, without letting it roll. They are alternating, as quickly as they can, one foot on the top of the ball and one foot on the ground.

Pendulums   Players stand with their feet slightly wider than shoulder-width apart, with the ball in between their feet. They knock the ball back and forth across the same strip of grass with the inside of their feet. The movement is like a clock pendulum, but players should have a slight bend in their knees so the movement is in their legs, not from the waist.

L-Turns   For L-turns (see figure 3.3), players start with the ball 6 to 12 inches (15 to 30 cm) in front of the right foot. They pull the ball back with the bottom of the right foot and pivot on the left foot 90 degrees to the right. After they pivot, they push the ball out to the right (or in front of them) with the inside of the right foot. Then they catch the ball as it is moving away from them with the left foot. To repeat it going the other way, they pull the ball back with the left foot, pivot on the right foot to the original start position, and push the ball with the inside of the left foot. To complete the move they catch the ball with the right foot. They can move back and forth continuously, which is a repetitive L. This is a great activity for practicing staying light on their feet because the players need to hop slightly when pivoting and switching feet.

V-Turns   For V-turns (see figure 3.4), players start with the ball 6 to 12 inches (15 to 30 cm) in front of the left foot. They pull the ball back with the sole of the left foot at a slight angle, moving the ball towards the center of the body. After slightly hopping while switching feet, they will use the inside of the right foot to push the ball out away from the body at an angle to complete the shape of a V. To repeat the move going the other way, instruct players to catch (stop) the ball with the bottom of the

Figure 3.3   For the L-turn, a player (*a*) pulls the ball back with the bottom of the right foot, (*b*) pivots on the left foot 90 degrees to the right, and (*c*) pushes the ball out to the right with the inside of the right foot. The player then repeats the skill starting with the left foot.

Figure 3.4   For the V-turn, a player (*a*) pulls the ball back with sole of left foot, (*b*) hops slightly to switch feet, and (*c*) uses the inside of right foot to push ball out to complete shape of V. The player then repeats the skill starting with the right foot.

right foot and then pull it back at an angle toward the center of the body. Then they push the ball out at an angle with the inside of the left foot to finish the V.

Dribbling in Confined Spaces

When dribbling in a confined space or an area with lots of other players around, players should follow four basic principles:

1. Keep the ball moving. When the ball stops, the opponent has an opportunity to step in and try to win possession.
2. Keep the ball within reach. The player with the ball must keep it within reach to avoid turning it over to the opposition.
3. Find space to safely dribble. This is the best way to keep the ball away from everyone else. The best way to find space is to look around.
4. Keep the head up. If players dribble with their heads down, staring at the ball, they will not see the spaces that are opening up around them, and they will not see their opponents prowling around and waiting for the chance to attack.

Once you have introduced your players to the principles of playing in tight spaces, you can show them some basic moves to use for changing directions and getting away from pressure. The following four basic moves can be performed while dribbling in a tight area or when players realize they need to turn back to where they originally came from.

Each of these moves provides a way for players to make a 180-degree turn, so if they are dribbling down the field they can quickly change direction and go back the other way. Players may need to perform one of these moves when they are heading toward the sideline or end line, if they realize they are dribbling into pressure, when they are going toward their own end and need to quickly turn around, or if they see their parents about to take their picture and want to escape the camera.

These skills can be practiced with or without pressure. You can incorporate them into your warm-up and assign them for take-home challenges. The more the players practice these types of moves, the more natural they will become in game situations. Again, have the players start slowly like turtles and then speed up like cheetahs as they become more comfortable with the move.

Inside Turn   To perform an inside turn (see figure 3.5), players move the ball forward with a dribble or two, then step with the plant foot (the pivot foot—not the one on the ball), placing it just ahead of the ball so the ball is to the outside of the plant foot. Then they pivot 180 degrees toward the ball, turning back to face the direction from which they just came. As they pivot, the players use the inside of the other foot to push in the direction they are now facing and then immediately follow after the ball so it stays within reach. For example, if a player is going to turn the ball with the inside of the right foot, the player should step with the left foot in front of the ball so the ball is to the outside of the left foot. Then the player should pivot on the left foot toward the ball, swinging the right leg around counterclockwise, and use the inside of the right foot to push the ball into space.

Figure 3.5   For an inside turn, a player (*a*) steps ahead of the ball with the plant foot, (*b*) pivots, and (*c*) kicks with the inside of the other foot.

Outside Turn   For an outside turn (see figure 3.6), players dribble the ball forward and then place the plant foot just ahead of the ball so the ball is on the inside of the plant foot. Players then rotate 180 degrees toward the ball, pivoting on the plant foot. With the outside of the other foot, they push the ball in the direction they are now facing and immediately follow the ball so it is always under control and within reach. For example, to turn the ball with the outside of the right foot, a player should step with the left foot to the left side of the ball and turn the right foot back toward the ball. Then the player can push the ball with the outside of the right foot, turn clockwise, and accelerate into space with the ball.

Figure 3.6   For an outside turn, a player (*a*) steps ahead of the ball with the plant foot and pivots, and then the player (*b*) pushes the ball with the outside of the other foot.

Drag-Back   On a drag-back (see figure 3.7), players dribble the ball forward, then place the plant foot next to the ball. (The ball will be on the inside of the plant foot.) Next, they place the bottom of the other foot on top of the ball and pull the ball backward underneath the body. As the ball is rolling, they should open the shoulder on the same side as the pulling foot (turning away from the plant foot) and pivot 180 degrees on the plant foot so the ball is now rolling in front of them. As they turn, they will lose contact with the ball for a brief second, so instruct the players to keep their eyes on the ball. When the turn is complete, players should regain contact with the ball, push it in the direction they were just coming from, and continue to follow the ball.

For example, to do a drag-back with the right foot, players should place the left foot next to the ball. Then they should place the bottom of the right foot on top of the ball and pull it back underneath them. They turn 180 degrees clockwise, pivoting on the left foot. The right leg hangs in the air as they turn, losing contact briefly with the ball. When the turn is complete, they should regain contact with the right foot and push the ball forward in the direction they just came from.

Figure 3.7   For a drag-back, a player (*a*) places the bottom of the nonplant foot on top of the ball, (*b*) drags the ball under the body with the other foot, and (*c*) pivots on the plant foot to head in the opposite direction.

Cruyff   The Cruyff is named for one of the greatest players in the world, Johan Cruyff. He led his club team, Ajax, to many championships and was named European Footballer of the Year three times in the 1970s. His best move was a turn in which he would pull the ball behind him, turn 180 degrees, and leave defenders still lunging for the ball. To complete a Cruyff (see figure 3.8), players push the ball forward and fake a kick with the inside of one foot, but instead of kicking the ball, they reach past the ball and use the inside of the same foot to pull the ball back underneath the body and change directions.

If a player is standing (planted) on the left foot, the player swings the right foot as if preparing to strike the ball. Instead of kicking the ball, the player moves the right foot past the outside of the ball and turns it so the inside of the right foot is now in front of the ball. This is an awkward pose because one foot is planted facing forward and the other foot is sideways, with the toe pointing toward the plant foot side. The player uses the inside of the right foot to push the ball back under the body and just in front of the plant foot. The player continues the motion to the left (counterclockwise), pivoting 180 degrees, regaining control of the ball, and moving into space while keeping the ball under control and within reach.

Figure 3.8   For a Cruyff, a player fakes a kick with one foot but instead (*a*) moves this foot around the ball with the toe pointed inward and then pushes the ball underneath the body. The player then (*b*) pivots 180 degrees on the plant foot to reverse the dribbling direction.

Moving Forward

When there is space in front of the player with the ball, it is not as important that he keep the ball within immediate reach. In fact, he will likely run much faster without the ball at his feet. Keep in mind that the ball is probably an *obstacle* for most of your players. They will often look like a cross between a penguin and a baby giraffe while dribbling the ball with the inside of their feet. So, if a player is attacking open space, encourage him to push the ball slightly ahead and then follow. Pushing the ball forward with the tops of the feet will help players maintain the most natural running form. This does *not* mean they should kick and run. A player dribbling the ball must still keep it close enough that opponents can't get it, and he should be able to reasonably stop or change directions while still maintaining possession.

Taking On an Opponent

The really fun part (or the completely scary part) of dribbling is taking on an opponent one versus one. Obviously, the objective is for the player with the ball to get past the player without the ball. The keys to success here are deception, ball control, and quickness. Deception is convincing the opponent that one thing is about to happen when, in fact, something else is going to happen. Most young players have no problem with deception because they, themselves, rarely know what they are going to do. An effective fake doesn't have to be complicated. Any movement that gets the opponent to lean in the wrong direction or hesitate to make a play is all that is needed.

Ball control is an often neglected aspect of one-versus-one attacking. Unfortunately, a phenomenal move or explosive speed is typically wasted if the player can't control the ball. When approaching the opponent, the attacking player should keep the ball close to her feet, and the attacker should try to make sure the ball remains in motion (it is harder for the opponent to hit a moving target). As the attacking player completes a hesitation, a move, or just a turning of the shoulders and hips, she should push the ball past the opponent, but not so far that possession is in jeopardy.

Quickness doesn't have to mean speed. A player who is slow can still use a change of pace to get by the defender. The attacker may slow a little when approaching the opponent. Then, just as the defender is getting ready to challenge, the offensive player should change direction and quickly move past the opponent.

Dribbling against an opponent in the open field can be one of the most fun and exciting parts of the game, but becoming comfortable in a one-versus-one situation takes a lot of time and practice. Introduce these moves individually during the first few practices. Some kids are intimidated by the idea that everyone is watching them, and they may think they will let their teammates down if they lose the ball. Help them become more comfortable with the ball at their feet by allowing them to practice without pressure, or in other words without an opponent. They can dribble in space or attack a cone or a parent helper. Encourage players to take chances in practice, and remind them that it's okay to fall down while trying a new skill.

The following moves can be used when a player with the ball is attacking an opposing player. The goal is to use the move to get the opponent to commit to one side or hesitate while the attacking player pushes the ball by and continues down the field. Encourage your players to practice these moves at home.

Matthews   To complete the Matthews (see figure 3.9), named for English star Stanley Matthews, players dribbling the ball fake in one direction and then quickly move in the other direction. The move, completed with just one foot, is a slight push across the body with the inside of the foot, followed by a push into space with the outside of that same foot. The player can make a slight shoulder fake with the first push to help sell the

Figure 3.9   For a Matthews, a player (a) uses the inside of one foot to fake movement or slightly move the ball in one direction and then (b) uses the outside of the same foot to move the ball the opposite direction.

move. For example, a player dribbling toward an opponent could take a quick touch with the inside of the left foot and nudge the ball across the body to the right. The player should lean the left shoulder in the same direction. The player should then quickly move the ball back to the left with the outside of the left foot. (The left foot will not touch the ground during the actual move.) The player then quickly follows the ball into the open space.

Stepover   Players can complete a stepover (see figure 3.10) while dribbling forward with the ball. The player makes a fake in one direction and then plays the ball in the other direction. Starting with the ball slightly in front of them, players move one foot around the outside of the ball so that both feet are now on the same side of the ball. Players then quickly push the ball forward at an angle with the outside of the same foot (the one that just went around the ball). So, if a player wishes to attack to the right, he dribbles forward slightly to the left. Then he quickly moves his right foot counterclockwise around the outside of the ball, so the right foot is next to the left foot. He then uses the outside of his right foot to push the ball forward at an angle to the right and accelerates into space.

Figure 3.10   For a stepover, a player (*a*) steps around the ball with one foot and (*b*) uses the outside of the same foot to move the ball forward.

Scissors　　The movement for performing the scissors is similar to the stepover, but the foot moves the opposite way around the ball. To perform a scissors (see figure 3.11), players quickly step around the ball, moving from the inside to the outside of the ball. Then, they shift their weight to the foot that just moved around the ball so they can push the ball away from the body with the outside of the other foot. They follow the ball into the open space. For example, to attack to the right, a player moves the left foot counterclockwise from the inside to the outside of the ball. The player quickly shifts weight to the left foot so he can now use the outside of the right foot to push the ball forward at an angle to the right and accelerate into space.

Figure 3.11　　For a scissors, a player (*a*) steps one foot from the inside to the outside of the ball, (*b*) shifts weight to the foot that just stepped, and (*c*) uses the outside of the opposite foot to move the ball forward into space.

Drill 1 Ball Hog

Skill warm-up, skill training

EQUIPMENT
Lots of balls; 1 cone for every player

PLAYING AREA
Adjust based on number of players and age of the players

PURPOSE
Teaching quick turns with the ball and dribbling at speed under control

PROCEDURE
Arrange cones in a circle, and assign each player to a cone. Each player has a safe zone around the outside of the cone. Start with players at their cones and all of the balls in the middle of the playing area. On your command, all the players run into the ceter and try to bring as many balls as they can back to their safe zone, dribbling one ball out at a time.

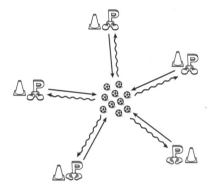

MODIFICATIONS
Players must use just the right or just the left foot. Or players can take a ball from a teammate if it isn't in the teammate's safe zone.

Drill 2 Traffic Cop

Skill warm-up, skill training, pregame warm-up

EQUIPMENT
1 ball for every player; cones to create a grid

PLAYING AREA
Square grid 15 × 15 yards to 30 × 30 yards (14 × 14 m to 27 × 27 m) depending on number of players

PURPOSE
Teaching players how to dribble in traffic, turn with the ball, and use dribbling moves

PROCEDURE
Each player dribbles a ball inside the grid and obeys the traffic cop (coach). Command the players to start, stop, turn, find space, do moves, slow down, speed up, pull over, and so on.

Drill 3 Sharks and Minnows

Skill warm-up, skill training, fun competition

EQUIPMENT
1 ball for every player; enough cones to create sidelines (or if on a field, you could use the area from the sideline to the side of the penalty box)

PLAYING AREA
Adjust according to the number of players; allow at least 3 yards between players and have them dribble 15 to 25 yards

PURPOSE
Teaching dribbling at game speed and attacking moves

PROCEDURE
Players (the minnows) line up side by side. Each player starts with a ball. The coach or a chosen player (the shark) stands in the middle of the playing area. On your signal, the players dribble across the playing field while the shark tries to steal the balls or knock them out of bounds. Players who lose their ball become sharks.

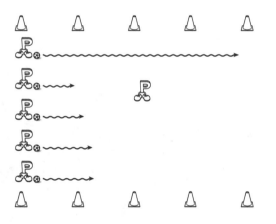

MODIFICATIONS
Players who become sharks can link arms or hold hands when trying to get the minnows. This creates one big shark that can cover more field space, making it more challenging for the minnows to get across the field.

Drill 4 Obstacle Course

Skill warm-up, skill training, fun competition

EQUIPMENT
1 ball for every player

PLAYING AREA
About 1/3 to 1/2 of a field

PURPOSE
Teaching players to dribble under control, dribble into open space, and turn with the ball

PROCEDURE
Set up a soccer obstacle course around the field or practice area using cones, corner flags, small goals, and so on. Get creative if you can, using benches, trash cans, parents, or other available items. The players line up at the starting line and go on command through the course. Allow adequate time in between players so they don't run into one another. Have fun with this! Mix in opportunities for the players to dribble in tight situations and to dribble with speed into space.

Drill 5 Knockout

Skill warm-up, skill training, fun competition

EQUIPMENT
1 ball for every player; cones to create a grid

PLAYING AREA
Square grid 10 × 10 yards to 20 × 20 yards (9 × 9 m to 18 × 18 m) depending on number of players

PURPOSE
Teaching players to dribble in traffic and turn with the ball

PROCEDURE
Each player dribbles a ball around inside the grid and tries to kick other players' soccer balls out of the grid. Players who lose their balls must leave the playing area. The last player with a ball in the grid wins.

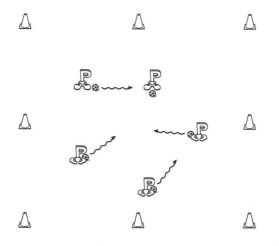

MODIFICATIONS
As players are knocked out, you can adjust the cones to shrink the field size. Another option is to allow players to reenter, but they get a point each time they do. At the end of the drill, the player with the low score wins.

Drill 6 Mirror Mirror

Skill training

EQUIPMENT
1 ball for every player; 1 cone for every 2 players

PLAYING AREA
An area 10 × 3 yards (9 × 3 m) for each pair of players

PURPOSE
Teaching players to dribble under control and turn with the ball

PROCEDURE
Each player should have a ball and a partner. Line up players so that the partners are on opposite sides of a cone, facing one another. Each player should be 3 to 5 yards (3 to 5 m) from the cone. On your command, the players dribble toward the cone, then turn (using one of the moves they've learned) and dribble back to their starting point.

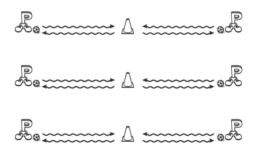

COACHING POINTS
Be sure players get close enough to the defender (cone) to make the turn as realistic as possible. However, they should allow enough room to be successful. They should not touch the cone.

MODIFICATIONS
Progress to attacking moves and have the players attack the cone, complete a move, and advance forward to where the partner started. To avoid crashes, make sure both partners go to the right or both go to the left of the cone.

Drill 7 Father Time

Skill training

EQUIPMENT
1 ball for every player; 13 cones

PLAYING AREA
Large circle, 10 to 20 yards (9 to 18 m) in diameter, with 12 cones representing the numbers 1 to 12 on a clock and the remaining cone in the center of the circle

PURPOSE
Teaching players to dribble under control and turn with the ball

PROCEDURE
For this drill, players need to know the position of numbers on a clock. Line all the players up at the top of the clock (12 o'clock). Players dribble, one at a time, toward the center of the clock. When the player starts dribbling, call out a time (1 to 12). The player dribbles straight to the middle of the clock and then turns sharply with the ball and dribbles to the time you called out. When he gets to that cone, he uses a 180-degree turn to go back to the center and then cuts straight up to 12 o'clock to finish. Then the next player goes.

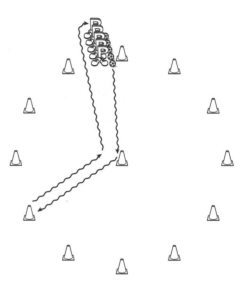

MODIFICATIONS
Place players at the top and bottom of the clock or the top, bottom, right, and left. The clock for each line is turned so they are each at 12 o'clock. In other words, 12 o'clock for one line would be 6 o'clock for another line. One player from each line goes each time.

Drill 8 Intersection

Skill training, pregame warm-up

EQUIPMENT
1 ball for every player; 4 cones

PLAYING AREA
Square grid 5 x 5 yards to 15 x 15 yards (5 x 5 m to 14 x 14 m) depending on number of players

PURPOSE
Teaching players to dribble under control, speed up and slow down with the ball, and complete 180-degree turns

PROCEDURE
Players line up with their balls on the sides of the grid. Make sure there are players on all four sides and that they are not directly across from one another. On command, the players dribble as quickly as possible straight across the grid and back. Players may speed up or slow down, but they must dribble straight ahead in their lanes.

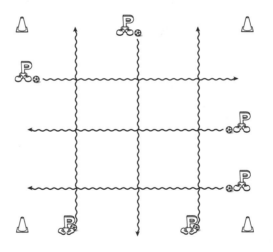

MODIFICATIONS
Restrict the foot or surface of the foot that the players are using. Make the grid smaller, and have the players go back and forth more than once in a turn. Keep track of accidents or lane violations.

Drill 9 Gates

Skill training, team training

EQUIPMENT
1 ball for every 2 players; 12 to 24 cones

PLAYING AREA
Square grid 20 × 20 yards to 35 × 35 yards (18 × 18 m to 32 × 32 m) depending on age group

PURPOSE
Teaching players to dribble under control, turn with the ball, and avoid traffic (opponents) by keeping their heads up

PROCEDURE
Inside the grid, randomly set up gates with pairs of cones about 2 yards (2 m) apart. Players are paired up; one will work inside the grid while the other stands on the outside counting and cheering. On command, the players inside the grid try to dribble their balls through as many gates as possible in a set time. Players can dribble through the gates from either side, but they can't go through the same gate twice in a row.

MODIFICATIONS
Restrict the players to using just one foot, or have them switch feet with each gate crossed. Have players enter a gate, complete a 180-degree turn, and exit the same gate to get a point. Have the partners act as defenders trying to stop them from getting through the gates.

Drill 10 Individual Attacking Scrimmage

Team training, games

EQUIPMENT
Several balls; pinnies; 12 cones

PLAYING AREA
Small field with goals or cones set up for goals 2 to 4 yards (2 to 4 m) wide

PURPOSE
Teaching players to find and attack open space and take players on 1v1

PROCEDURE
Players scrimmage (without goalkeepers) 3v3 to 7v7 depending on the age group. Award players one point for beating, or getting past, an opponent while dribbling. Award one point for a goal and two points for a goal scored by a player dribbling the ball through the goal. Play for 5 to 15 minutes. Consider moving players into different positions halfway through the scrimmage.

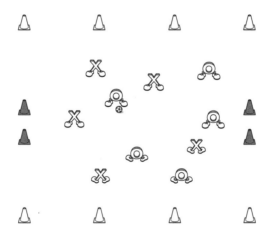

MODIFICATIONS
Play with regular goals and goalkeepers. Require players to beat an opponent while dribbling before they are allowed to pass or shoot.

The Coach's Clipboard

✔ Feet, feet, feet! Make your players use their feet, not their hands, at all times when working with the ball.

✔ Create opportunities for success, especially early on, by allowing players to learn to dribble in slow motion, without defenders, and with lots of space.

✔ Encourage players to use all surfaces of both feet.

✔ No toes! Help players learn to dribble correctly so they do not develop bad habits.

✔ Teach fast footwork moves to help players become comfortable with the ball at their feet.

✔ Remind players to stay light on their feet, turn or complete a footwork move as quickly as possible, and accelerate with the ball after the move.

✔ When dribbling in traffic, players should keep the ball moving, keep the ball within reach, keep the head up, look for space, and then dribble into that space.

✔ When dribbling into space, players should use the top of the foot to push the ball forward and then follow it.

✔ The keys to successfully taking on an opponent are deception, control, and quickness.

✔ Help the players master at least one attacking move they can use to beat an opponent.

Teaching Passing and Receiving Skills With 10 Simple Drills

Every player (hopefully) wants to touch the ball during the game. Most players will want to touch it often, and some might even yell and scream when they don't get the ball. This is why beehive soccer is so common. It is pretty straightforward: *I want the ball, so I am going to go get it—even if my teammate has it.* Kids are smart and often determined, but they are not necessarily productive in their actions.

Parents have their own wish as well; they want their kid to touch the ball all the time. They are not as frank as a 5-year-old, so they yell, "Boot it!" to the kid with the ball, hoping that the ball gets kicked to their son or daughter. What they are forgetting is that the ball may very well get booted, but there is a slim chance that it will end up at their child's foot.

Luckily the soccer gods have created another, more efficient method of moving the ball among players—the pass. For the pass to work, a player must be willing and able to relinquish control of the ball, and another player must be able to receive it. These two skills are necessary to execute all tactical strategy. They make the game beautiful and get coaches, like you, excited! Teams who can pass have several advantages over teams who spend most of their time dribbling.

First, passing teams get less tired because the ball is moving more than the players; they are using their resources better. Now, we don't want to mislead you. If you have a completely unfit team, you cannot solve all your problems by passing; it still takes work to move into the proper space to receive the pass and energy to execute successful distribution of the ball. The good thing is that players without the ball don't have to run around trying to use their psychic powers to figure out what their dribbling teammate is going to do with the ball.

A second benefit of passing is that the ball gets stolen less by the other team. *Wait*, you may be thinking, *what about all those passes that get intercepted?* While your team is learning how to effectively pass, they may lose the ball to the other team, but not as much as an inexperienced dribbler will. This is how it works: Your player has the ball. As the opponent approaches, your player passes the ball to a teammate. Now the opponent must turn and go get the ball from that person. As the opponent approaches, the teammate who now has the ball passes it again—kind of like a game of keep-away. The person in the middle (the opponent) always ends up getting tired and frustrated before the attackers do (this is why it is so entertaining to play and watch games with quality passing).

A third advantage for passing teams is that players have more fun playing because they get to be constantly involved in the game. The ultimate advantage is that teams who pass have better opportunities to score and therefore an increased chance to win. Have we convinced you that passing and receiving are the keys to success?

Now before we discuss the fundamentals, let's talk about a few things that will help you teach passing and receiving more effectively.

- **Players don't *boot* the ball.** Players kick, pass, shoot, or clear the ball. *Booting* the ball typically involves kicking the ball with the toes or kicking the ball randomly. Do not let your players do this. If you find the parents on your team yelling this not-so-helpful instruction from the sideline, remind them that booting the ball typically results in turning over the ball to the other team. Let them know that you are working on the fundamentals of passing and that (if they must yell) you would rather they yell, "Pass it!" instead of "Boot it!"

- **Passing is done with a purpose.** Teach your players early in the learning process that they should have a purpose when they kick the ball. Even if they cannot correctly execute the pass, it is still important that they know what they intend to do with the ball.

- **The passer has the treasure.** The passer is the most valued person on the field because she possesses the ball (and probably doesn't want to get rid of it). This player's role is to decide what type of pass to use and when to execute the pass.

- **The receiver is on the other end of the pass.** The role of this player is to move into a space where the passer can find him and then to handle the ball when it is played.
- **Players should use both feet.** Typically players have one foot that they like to use the most—the dominant foot. It typically mirrors the writing hand. Although it is okay to let them use the foot that is more natural to them, encourage them to practice with both feet. Design your drills to allow players to practice dribbling, passing, receiving, and shooting with both feet.

As with dribbling, encourage your players to use all surfaces of both feet to pass—except their toes. *No toes!* The inside of the foot is the most accurate way to pass, but the top of the foot (at the laces) allows for more distance. The top of the foot can be used to get the ball in the air, while the outside of the foot allows for curving a pass or executing a short, deceptive pass.

Designing a Passing Practice

As a coach, you will likely find passing to be the most enjoyable aspect of the game. Certainly it is fun to watch the players develop their moves and dribbling skills. They will all be thrilled about shooting and scoring goals. But the teamwork involved in quality passing is rewarding, because everyone on the team can benefit at any time. When a team plays with passing as a priority, the energy and excitement level of players without the ball will often match that of the players with the ball. Use this excitement as motivation as you introduce your players to the basics of passing.

Most of your players will have little experience passing the ball with their feet. Like dribbling, it is often second nature to pass with our hands, but we feel like a fish out of water when passing with our feet. Passing is a crucial skill in the game of soccer, so you will need to have your team practice it again and again. Figure 4.1 provides a sample passing practice. You can use different drills to maintain interest and create challenging situations.

Passing is a great skill to use as the basis of take-home challenges, and believe it or not, players don't necessarily need a partner to practice passing. A wall or garage door (with permission from Mom or Dad) can be used as the receiver. Players can pass against the wall, receive the ball, and then pass again. Parents also like the wall because it eliminates embarrassing moments of awkward passing for them. If Mom and Dad

Figure 4.1 Sample Passing Practice Plan

Coach: _____ Date: _____

Time: _____

Age group: <u>Any</u>   Theme: <u>Passing</u>

Practice part	Duration	Equipment	Activity or drill
Skill warm-up	10-15 min.	1 ball	*Tunnel passing* (see page 82) *Stretching*
Skill training	10-15 min.	1 ball for every 2 players	*No-hand catch* (see page 84)
Water break			
Team training	10-15 min.	1 ball, cones to set up grid boundaries, pinnies	*Possession grids* (see page 90)
Water break			
Games	10-15 min.	1 ball (and a few extras off to the side), pinnies, cones for field, and 2 goals	*Scrimmage:* Divide players into 2 even teams and play a game emphasizing passing and receiving technique. You may restrict the number of touches a player can take before passing or award points for a set number of consecutive passes as well as for goals scored.
Cool-down	5 min.	All the balls used in practice	*Equipment passing:* Have the players jog around to collect the stray balls from practice (if there aren't many strays, send some balls out around the field while the players are collecting the cones and pinnies). Players should pass the balls in to you. Challenge the players to use the smallest number of passes possible, so the balls that are far away may require a driven ball and then a short push pass as the players get closer. *Stretch* when finished.

From L. Blom and T. Blom, 2009, *Survival Guide for Coaching Youth Soccer* (Champaign, IL: Human Kinetics).

are willing to play, a little keep-away from Fido or passing around the trees in the yard is a fun outdoor activity the family can do together. You can assign a variety of take-home challenges that involve passing. One example is to challenge players to pass the ball 20 times with the inside of the right foot, top of the right foot, inside of the left foot, and top of the left foot during the course of the week.

Because passing with the feet is awkward and takes time to master, do not expect your players to learn the skill at game speed. Use the following guidelines to create a passing progression that will set up successful experiences for your players. Players will be more likely to want to continue learning how to pass and less likely to become frustrated and resort to using their toes if they take it one step at a time.

- Practice without the ball. Let the players learn how to properly move their legs before adding a ball so they don't have to worry about where the ball is going. They might feel silly at first; do it with them and have fun with it.

- Practice passing with a ball from a standing position. This isn't gamelike, but that is okay for now. Have the players hit toward a stationary target.

- Practice passing from a standing position toward a moving target (such as a teammate or coach who is jogging toward or beside the passer). This adds a new element of skill.

- Once they feel comfortable with the passing mechanics, encourage players to dribble before passing to a target.

- The final step involves designating a space where the players with the ball dribble as they prepare to pass and the players without the ball jog around waiting to receive it in order to simulate game conditions. You can add defenders and goals to attack when appropriate. (Sometimes goals distract players from the chosen task, so be careful when you add them into a drill.)

Teaching Passing

Different types of passes can be used depending on the purpose of the pass. *Here they go again*, you think. *Isn't the purpose to get the ball from one player to another?* Yes, that's correct, and for young, inexperienced players (4 to 8 years old), this is the only purpose they will need to worry about while playing. As players develop their skills, however, they will need to understand the other types of passes. You should understand the three main factors that determine the purpose of a pass so you can help your players choose when to use the different types of passes.

The first factor is how hard to pass the ball—in other words, how much pace, speed, or power to put into the kick. The more distance there is between the passer and the receiver, the more pace must be put on the pass (say that 10 times fast). The second factor is the need for accuracy. All passes need some accuracy (we don't want any spectators to get hurt), but some require more than others. The closer the opponent is to the receiver, the more accurate the pass needs to be. Sometimes it is helpful to play the ball into the space in front of the receiver; in this case less accuracy is required. The final factor is the timing of the pass. The passer must decide when and where the receiver wants to get the ball. Does he want it at his feet? Does she want it out in front of her so she can run onto it? Should the ball be played as quickly as possible, or does the teammate need time to create space from a defender?

This probably sounds like a lot of information for young players to process. To simplify, start them with the rule that passing to an open teammate equals a good choice. The rest will come with time and well-planned practices. Look for opportunities to stop a scrimmage and point out open players and good passing options. As far as types of passes, young players will primarily pass with the inside of the foot (push pass, short pass), but as they develop, they'll need to know the driven pass (long pass), cross, chip, and wall pass (one-two pass, give-and-go).

Inside-of-the-Foot Pass

The inside of the foot is used to move the ball with accuracy a short to moderate distance. This pass is the most important pass and should be used often, so give your players plenty of opportunities to practice it frequently. As with all passes, the entire leg is involved in passing the ball. Instruct the players to swing the leg from the hip rather than just from the knee. The quadriceps (thigh) is the biggest muscle group in the leg, so players should use that part of the leg.

To perform the inside-of-the-foot pass, a player stands facing the ball, which should be between the player and the target. The player places the nonkicking foot, or plant foot, about 3 to 5 inches (8 to 13 cm) to the

Barefoot Basics

During the initial stages of learning how to pass, have your players take off their shoes and socks so they can more clearly see and feel the point of contact with the ball. Players typically think this change of routine is fun, although they might say, at first, that it hurts to kick without their shoes. This is not a good idea on a rainy day or on a rocky field or with players who shower infrequently!

side of the ball, with the toes pointed toward the passing target (see figure 4.2a). Both knees should be slightly bent. (The stance should be comfortable—legs like slightly cooked spaghetti rather than uncooked spaghetti.) The middle of the body should also face the target. Tell kids to keep their belly buttons facing the target. The arms should be at the side of the body to be used for balance. They should not be out to the sides like a helicopter.

The player plants the nonkicking foot and takes a short backswing with the kicking leg, opening the hip so the inside of the foot faces the ball (figure 4.2a). The foot should be slightly off the ground. The player should strike the middle of the ball with the middle of the inside of the foot (closer to the ankle bone than the toe) to send it in the targeted direction as shown in figure 4.2b. Instruct players to strike the ball with the logo on the inside of their cleats. At contact, the angle of the foot should be locked, with the heel down and toes up.

Young players should keep their eyes on the ball as they strike it. Encourage them to find a mark on the ball that they want to hit as they make contact. As players master the skill, keeping an eye on the ball is less important, but novice players need to watch the ball or they may end up on the ground after pulling a Charlie Brown. The foot should follow through toward the target in a fluid motion. Because of this smooth follow-through, this pass is often referred to as a push pass. If the ball is struck properly, it should have some topspin. After the pass, players should look up so they can follow the play. As players become more comfortable with this skill, encourage them to dribble and then pass without stopping between skills.

Figure 4.2 Proper technique for executing an inside pass.

Driven Pass

The driven pass is a hard, off-the-ground pass that is made with the top of the foot. This pass allows players to move the ball with power a moderate to long distance, although it sacrifices some accuracy. It differs from the inside-of-the-foot pass in two main ways: (1) Contact is made with the top of the foot (laces) instead of the inside of the foot, and (2) the emphasis is power rather than accuracy.

The approach to this pass is important. Because power is key, players cannot correctly drive the ball if they are in a stationary position before making contact. However, Excited Eric does not need to take a running start from the parking lot to complete this pass. Teach players to use a three-step approach, starting with a step from the nonkicking foot. They should approach the ball from a slight angle, about 35 degrees, and comfortably bend both knees slightly. They should keep their eyes on the ball.

As the nonkicking foot is planted about 4 to 6 inches (10 to 15 cm) to the side of the middle of the ball, players will take a backswing, from the hip, with the kicking leg (see figure 4.3a). On the kicking foot, the ankle is locked and the toe is pointed down toward the ground. The toe should just scrape the grass as the laces of the shoe strike the middle of the ball (figure 4.3b). Instruct players to keep the knee over the ball as they strike through it. Then they should continue to follow through after striking the ball.

Figure 4.3 Proper technique for executing a driven pass.

Cross

The cross is a driven pass that is sent from the side of the field to the center of the field, typically to create a scoring opportunity. The purpose is to move the ball with speed in the air from one area of the field to another. Pace is also important with a cross so that the opponents and goalkeeper don't intercept the service. Now, if you have a little Beckham on your team, just let him demonstrate and teach this technique to the rest of your team, while you sit back and relax. Otherwise, here are the steps to learning how to cross the ball.

Typically the laces are used to cross the ball, but if a player can get enough power on a cross with the inside of the foot, then that works too. Therefore, the steps of this pass are very similar to the driven pass except for the last touch before contact. As with all passes, the ball should be between the kicker and the target. But because the cross is used when players are by the sideline, the target is to the side instead of in front of the kicker.

Instruct players to take their last dribble toward the middle of the field in order to get the ball between them and their target. This will decrease the number of times that a cross is sent out of bounds or behind the goal. Once the kicker is facing the target, the next step is to push the ball slightly out in front of his body with that last dribble before kicking the ball (see figure 4.4*a*). As he does this, he wants to approach the ball from a slight angle, about 35 degrees, with the knees comfortably bent and his eyes on the ball. As the kicker plants his nonkicking foot about 4 to 6 inches (10 to 15 cm) toward the back of the ball, instruct him to take a backswing, from the hip, with the kicking leg (see figure 4.4*b*). Make sure the hip is turned toward the ball. On the kicking foot, the ankle is

Figure 4.4   Proper technique for executing a cross.

locked and the toe is pointed down toward the ground. The toe should just scrape the grass as the laces of the shoe strike the middle of the ball. Players should make contact with the top of the foot slightly below the center of the ball. As the kicker makes contact, he should lean the body back if he wishes wish to lift the ball into the air.

Chip Pass

The chip is a short, lofted (arc) pass used to clear an obstacle; the purpose is to move the ball over a defender (or two) or a goalkeeper in close range. This is a more advanced skill that is not used on a regular basis. It is very similar to a chip in golf, involving a quick, controlled swing with limited backswing and follow-through. Chipping is a good technique to use when the goalkeeper is out from the goal or a defender is between the passer and the receiver.

Players should place the nonkicking foot about 4 to 6 inches (10 to 15 cm) to the side of the ball and slightly behind it. Then they take a very short backswing with the kicking foot. They should angle the kicking foot down, like a wedge, and make contact with the front, top part of the foot below the center of the ball (see figure 4.5a). To lift the ball into the air, they should lean the body back slightly as they make contact with the ball. Instruct players to stop their follow-through quickly and bring the knee of the kicking leg straight up, giving the ball backspin (see figure 4.5b).

Figure 4.5　Proper technique for executing a chip.

Wall Pass

A wall pass is a quick inside-of-the-foot pass to a teammate who quickly returns the ball to the original passer. Wall passes are used to quickly move the ball around a defender with a teammate's help. As the player with the ball approaches an opponent, she plays a short, quick inside-of-the-foot pass to

Figure 4.6   Proper execution of a wall pass.

a teammate who is standing parallel to her (see figure 4.6). The teammate then plays a short, quick inside-of-the-foot pass (ideally with only one or two touches) behind the defender at a 45-degree angle, leading the original passer down the field. The original passer should move into the space behind the defender while waiting for the pass back from her teammate. This pass is also called a give-and-go because the passer gives the ball to a teammate and then goes into the space to get the ball back.

Passing With One and Two Touches

To teach this type of pass, you must be comfortable with the terms *first touch*, *second touch*, and *ultimate touch*. First touch is the first contact the player makes with the ball when receiving and settling. If she can do it in one motion, she has used one touch to settle the ball. Most beginning players need several touches to control the ball when first learning the skill. The second touch is the next contact the player makes with the ball after initially trying to receive it. Touches are counted up to the point the player passes the ball to someone else, which is the ultimate touch. Skilled players develop the ability to receive the ball and then pass it accurately with a minimal number of touches.

So for one-touch and two-touch passing, players receive a ball and pass it off with their first touch, or they take two touches—one to receive and settle the ball and one to pass it to a teammate. To control a pass from a teammate, players will initially need to take one or more touches before passing the ball because quite often the passes coming their way will be in their general vicinity rather than straight to their feet, or they will be bouncy rather than rolling gently along the turf. It is very challenging to receive and settle balls that are not accurately played smoothly on the ground.

Players need to feel comfortable both passing the ball immediately and controlling it before passing so that they decide which method to use based on the situation. However, you will typically find that beginning players will one-touch pass regardless of the situation. This does not mean your players have mastered the art of one-touch passing; it really means that either the players do not like the pressure of having the ball at their feet or they have fallen victim to the "boot it" commands from the stands. You want them to be somewhere between "hot potato," where players just kick the ball as if it were on fire, and "finders keepers, losers weepers," where they want to keep the ball as if it were their favorite toy. Encourage players to make purposeful passing decisions that help the team.

At first, to help your players overcome their fears of controlling the ball or overcome the boot-it mentality, you can require players to take a minimum number of touches before passing the ball. After they begin to feel comfortable, set up drills that work on one-touch passing as well. Moving the ball quickly can be a wonderful asset for a team. In some situations, such as a wall pass or when an opponent is approaching, players ideally use a one-touch pass because it is quick and does not allow the opponent time to get set up. Of course, the ultimate goal is to develop players who have the composure and wherewithal to make the best decision to find the most productive pass in a given situation and the ability to execute that pass.

Passing on Defense and Offense

Different passes are used depending on the half of the field the ball is in when passing. In the defensive half of the field, your players will feel more pressure because the ball is in front of their goal. Parents along the sidelines will often make them feel as if a live grenade is rolling toward their bunker, as they scream, "Kick it out, kick it out!" Although there is a sense of urgency, encourage your players to still pass with a purpose, as opposed to booting the ball or just kicking it out. When on defense, instruct your players to use long inside-of-the-foot, driven, or clearing passes most frequently. These passes require less accuracy, so they can be completed quickly as pressure from an opponent increases, but the players can still hit the ball in the general direction of their teammates. Players should also think about where they are passing the ball. Playing the ball down the sideline is a better choice than sending it into the middle of the field. Consider the outcome if the ball is mis-hit; obviously a turnover on the side of the field is less dangerous than one directly in front of your own goal.

In the offensive half of the field, there is more time to be creative. This is a place to take chances and be risky. Encourage your players to use inside-of-the foot passes, wall passes, chips, and crosses to create scoring opportunities. Passes that go between opponents into open space (often referred to as *through balls*) can lead teammates to a goal-scoring opportunity. Communication and timing are important when creating opportunities in the offensive end of the field. Also, positive communication from teammates and coaches is crucial in order for young players to become willing to take risks on the field.

Receiving a Pass

When a child comes home from school with a wonderful and creative pottery art project, parents are usually careful to treat it as a prized possession and praise their child's work (even if they're not sure what the lump of clay is supposed to be). In this situation and in soccer, it is incredibly important that the recipient fully understand the importance of his role in the situation. The player who receives a pass in soccer has been given a prized possession, and it is his responsibility to help his team maintain that possession.

There are several aspects of receiving a ball that can make the job more manageable. One is being aware that the ball is coming. If you are eagerly expecting the prized artwork of a 6-year-old, then your response will likely be gracious. If you're unprepared, you might hesitate or fumble for a bit before giving an appropriate response. The same is true in soccer. If players expect to get the ball, then they can be fully prepared to take control of it and to help the team hold on to it. If players are not expecting the ball, then fumbling around and guessing what to do next is a typical reaction. Tell your players to always expect to get the ball and to communicate. A pass should never be a surprise gift. Any time your team has the ball, all the players should prepare themselves as if they are going to get it next.

The players should work on being aware of the space around them and try to see what options they might have once they get the ball. The player with the ball and the teammates who want the ball should communicate with one another. At higher levels of soccer, this might be a hand motion, a point, a nod, or even just a look. At this level, the person who yells first or yells the loudest will likely get the ball. Help your players see that rather than just screaming the name of the player with the ball, it is more productive to give some direction to that player. "Out wide," "down the line," "drop," and "in the corner" are all common ways to tell the player with the ball where a good option is for a pass.

The player with the ball can simply call the name of the target to let her know that the ball is (hopefully) coming her way. After playing the ball, the passer should try to give another quick bit of information to let the recipient know whether she has time, should turn with the ball, or should play it back, or if a defender is close by. Tell your players, "Be an extra set of eyeballs for your teammates to help them learn how to communicate."

After preparing for the pass, the next step in receiving a pass is to get ready to control the ball. Ideally, the ball will be coming on the ground, and the player can receive the ball with the foot. Although it is important to be able to use all parts of the foot, the most common way to receive a pass is with the inside of the foot. This is the largest, easiest surface to cushion the ball with, and if you think about it, it is shaped perfectly for catching a soccer ball.

As the ball is coming, the recipient should present the inside of one foot while planting the other foot on the ground and bending the knees slightly (see figure 4.7). The idea is to cushion the ball as it comes in, much like an egg toss or water balloon contest. You could even do a water balloon toss at practice to emphasize the point of cushioning the ball when it comes in. As your players work on passing and receiving during practice, emphasize that the ball should stay close to the feet of

Figure 4.7 Proper technique for receiving a pass with the foot.

the recipient. The other team will likely recover a ball that bounces away. To practice this point, you can put a small boundary around the players and challenge them to stop the ball within that area.

Receiving the ball with other parts of the foot or other parts of the body follows the same principle as receiving the ball with the inside of the foot: Think water balloon. The most common parts of the body to use, other than the feet, are the thigh and chest. The player should position the surface that is receiving the ball in the ball's path (figure 4.8) and, with the knees slightly bent, cushion the impact of the ball. The goal is for the ball to come down right at the feet so the receiver can then dribble, pass, or shoot. This tactic should be incorporated into your practice, as the ball often ends up bouncing around the field as much as it does rolling along the grass. Although it is often attempted, receiving or trapping the ball with the shins, abdomen, or face should be discouraged.

The last step of receiving a pass is the "what now" part of the equation. The players are anticipating the pass, and they are ready to receive it and maintain possession. Encourage your players to look around all the time while they are moving on the field. They should be looking at where their teammates are, where the opponents are, and where there is space. If they are in the offensive end of the field, they should look to see where they are in relation to the goal.

Figure 4.8   Proper technique for receiving a pass with the chest.

CHECKers

The best way to alleviate the pressure of receiving a ball is for the players to give themselves more room to work. This is most often done by checking to the ball. When players check to the ball, they use a change of speed and a change of direction to quickly move to the ball and get away from any defenders. For example, a player on the offensive team may slowly move away from a teammate who has the ball. As the player without the ball moves, the opponent responsible for covering this player will likely move along with the player. As the player with the ball looks to make a pass, the player without the ball can quickly change direction and run toward the teammate with the ball. This quick movement is intended to catch the opponent off guard and create space for the offensive player. This technique is also effective when receiving a ball and trying to shoot before defenders have time to close down the space.

Before players receive a pass, they should have an idea of what their options are with the ball. Should they dribble? Is there an open teammate farther down the field? Is there a chance to get a good shot on goal? Asking young kids to be aware of everything around them when receiving a pass is a tall order. Be patient and understand that much of this progress will be learned and developed with time. The game is often the best teacher.

Drill 1 Marbles

Skill warm-up, skill training

EQUIPMENT
1 ball for every player, cones to mark grid boundaries

PLAYING AREA
At least a 25-yard (23 m) square; could be larger, just be sure to define a playing area

PURPOSE
Teaching players to accurately pass, using the proper passing technique without pressure from opponents

PROCEDURE
Players should be paired up, and each player should have a ball. The players in each pair should stand about 1 yard (1 m) apart. Player 1 attempts to pass his ball into Player 2's ball. After both balls stop rolling, Player 2 passes his ball into Player 1's ball. Each attempt is taken from where the balls stopped rolling from the previous attempt. If a ball goes outside of the playing area, have the players bring it back in. Each time a player hits

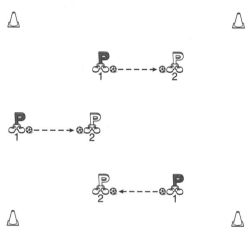

his partner's ball, he collects a point or a letter (similar to HORSE; you can use MARBLES or spell the team's name). The player who reaches the designated score or spelling wins the round. When players finish the round, have them find a new partner.

COACHING POINTS
Be sure that players are using the correct technique. Help players figure out how the pace of the pass affects the distance the opponent's ball travels. If they hit the opponent's ball with power, their own ball will not end up as close to their opponent's as when hit with a soft pass.

MODIFICATIONS
Dictate which foot players can use to pass the ball.

Drill 2 Tunnel Passing

Skill warm-up, skill training, pregame warm-up

EQUIPMENT
1 ball

PLAYING AREA
5 yards × 20 yards (5 m × 18 m)

PURPOSE
Teaching players how to develop quality first touches and accurate passes as well as how to move to receive the ball

PROCEDURE
Players line up in two lines. The first person in each line should face the other, and the lines should be 4 to 12 yards (4 to 11 m) apart. (The distance between the lines can increase with skill and strength.) The first player in one line passes to the first player in the other line. The player who passes the ball runs to the back of the opposite line. The first player in this line (who just received the pass) passes the ball back to the first player who is now at the front of the original line, and this process continues until you instruct the players to stop.

COACHING POINTS
Be sure players are using the correct passing and receiving technique. Remind them to receive the ball with the inside of the foot (careful with that water balloon!) and to use appropriate pace to get the ball to their teammate, keeping it under control.

MODIFICATIONS
Limit players to one or two touches. Require players to alternate which foot they receive and pass with.

Drill 3 Circle Passing

Skill warm-up, skill training, pregame warm-up

EQUIPMENT
1 to 3 balls

PLAYING AREA
Area large enough for all players to spread out in a circle for 5- to 10-yard (5 to 9 m) passes

PURPOSE
Teaching players to use proper passing technique, move to receive the ball, communicate with teammates, and follow the pass

PROCEDURE
One player starts with the ball at her feet. She calls the name of a teammate and passes the ball to that player. After passing the ball, she follows the pass and takes her teammate's place on the circle. The player receiving the ball moves to the ball, controls it, calls another teammate's name, and passes her the ball. The passer again follows the ball, and the drill continues in this manner.

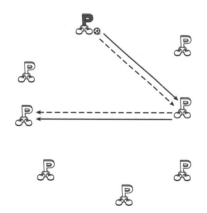

COACHING POINTS
Encourage proper passing and receiving technique. Require that players without the ball call the name of the player with the ball in order to receive it.

MODIFICATIONS
Once the team is comfortable moving one ball around the square, add a second and third ball to challenge the players.

Drill 4 No-Hand Catch

Skill warm-up, skill training, pregame warm-up

EQUIPMENT
1 ball for every 2 players

PLAYING AREA
Space for pairs of players to work together

PURPOSE
Teaching players to use proper techniques for receiving with foot, thigh, chest, and head

PROCEDURE
Partners should stand 4 to 8 yards (4 to 7 m) apart and face each other. They pass the ball with the inside of the foot back and forth using two touches: one to settle the ball and one to pass it back. Players then build on the basic drill with the following progression:

1. The players move closer, to a distance of about 1 to 2 yards (1 to 2 m apart). One player uses both hands to underhand serve the ball to the partner. At first, the server should toss the ball to the partner at just below knee height. The partner receives the ball out of the air with the inside of the foot and then passes the ball back on the ground. This partner should practice receiving the ball with the left and the right foot. After 30 to 45 seconds, the partners switch roles.

2. The server tosses the ball about waist high. The receiver uses the thigh to bring the ball down (see photo) and then uses the right or left foot to pass the ball back to the server. Switch roles after 30 to 45 seconds.

3. Partners practice using the chest to receive the ball. Switch roles after 30 to 45 seconds.

4. Players head the ball (see chapter 8) back to their partners. Switch roles after 30 to 45 seconds.

COACHING POINTS

Very young players or players who are having trouble serving the ball should stand side by side, with a little room between them, so you can move down the line serving the ball. This works well with three to five players. If you have more than that, recruit another adult to help you serve.

MODIFICATIONS

You can follow the order listed or modify the order if you want to focus on receiving with a specific body part.

Drill 5 Monkey in the Middle

Skill warm-up, skill training, pregame warm-up

EQUIPMENT
1 ball; cones to create a grid; 1 pinny for the "monkey"

PLAYING AREA
Square grid 10 × 10 yards to 15 × 15 yards (9 × 9 m to 14 × 14 m) (The outside players need enough room to make successful passes, but you do not want the monkey to run around and around. Make two grids if you have more than seven players.)

PURPOSE
Teaching proper passing technique when in a confined space, how to find open teammates, and how to productively move without the ball

PROCEDURE
Position four to six players along the sides of the grid and a defender (the monkey) in the middle. The players on the sides of the grid play keep-away against the defender. They are allowed to move around the grid but not through the inside. They can only move toward the inside to receive a ball and pass it off to someone else. If a player along the side of the grid loses possession to the defender or causes the ball to go outside of the grid, he switches places with the defender and becomes the new monkey.

COACHING POINTS
You might catch players standing still in the square. Encourage them to continuously move into position to support the teammate who has the ball. Instruct open players to move so the person with the ball can see them without an opponent in between.

MODIFICATIONS
To add variety to this drill, add a second defender, limit the number of touches for the players on the outside, or keep track of the number of successful passes for the players on the outside.

Drill 6 Add-On

EQUIPMENT
1 or 2 balls; 4 to 6 cones

PLAYING AREA
15- to 30-yard (14 to 27 m) grid, with cones used to mark the beginnings of four to six equally spaced lines forming a circle around the outside of the grid

PURPOSE
Teaching players to use proper passing and receiving technique by allowing players to focus on one specific aspect of passing and receiving at a time

PROCEDURE
Form four to six lines around the outside of the grid, with two or three players in each line. The first player in one of the lines should start with a ball at her feet. She passes to the first player in the next line and then runs to the back of that line. The player who receives the pass turns and plays the ball to the first person in the next line, and so on. Have the players pass to the line on the left (clockwise) if you want them to focus on using the left foot or

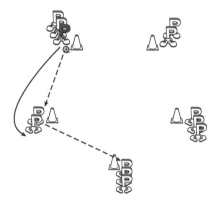

to the right (counterclockwise) to work on the right foot. If the players can handle it, add a second ball on the opposite side of the circle to minimize standing and waiting.

COACHING POINTS
You can use this drill to emphasize any of the following points, and you can add them on as players are ready (when they have demonstrated success with the current point).

1. Emphasize passing accurately using the inside of the foot, then following the pass.

2. Ask players to communicate to their teammates. Players with the ball should call the name of the teammate they are passing to. The player who is going to receive the ball should call for it before it is passed ("Yes, Jimmy" or "Feet, feet" lets Jimmy know the player is open to receive a pass and wants the ball played into the feet).

(continued)

3. Have players take a good first touch in the direction of the next line. The players should open their bodies up to the field, meaning they should stand so they can look at where the ball is coming from and where it is going without having to turn their bodies. When the ball comes in, the first touch should be a light touch of the ball in the direction of the next line, so the second touch can be a pass.

4. Tell players to move toward the ball to receive it. When a player passes the ball, the recipient of the pass should move to the ball rather than wait for it to come to her.

MODIFICATIONS
For older or more advanced players, you can add a few more points:

1. Have players check away from the pass, then move toward the ball. As the passer takes the first touch, the recipient should take several steps away from the passer, then quickly change directions back toward the ball when it is passed. The idea is to create space away from the defender.

2. Add a wall pass. Now when a player receives a ball, he will pass it back to the original passer, who should move toward him to receive it. The original passer plays the ball again, leading the receiver in the direction of the next line.

Drill 7 Blackjack (21)

EQUIPMENT
1 ball; enough cones to create a large grid and 2 goals

PLAYING AREA
Square grid 30 × 30 yards (27 × 27 m) or larger depending on the age and skill level; use cones to place the goals, 4 to 8 yards (4 to 7 m) wide, inside the grid

PURPOSE
Teaching accurate passing, moving without the ball, finding open teammates, and effective communication

PROCEDURE
Two teams of equal numbers of players try to maintain possession of the ball within the grid and pass the ball through either goal. The ball must be passed through the goal from one player to a teammate in order to score. Goals can be scored by kicking the ball through in either direction (there is no front or back to the goal). First team to 21 wins.

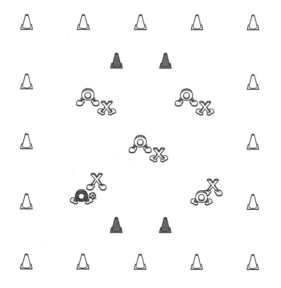

MODIFICATIONS
Play to a lower score to shorten the game. To spread the possessions around, limit the number of consecutive touches a player can make.

Drill 8 Possession Grids

Team training

EQUIPMENT
1 ball; cones to set up grid boundaries; pinnies

PLAYING AREA
Large grid 15 × 30 yards to 20 × 40 yards (14 × 27 m to 18 × 37 m), with cones dividing it into two square areas

PURPOSE
Teaching accurate passing, effective communication, moving with and without the ball, and transitioning from offense to defense

PROCEDURE
Divide players into two equal teams; players from both teams spread out on both sides of the grid. The team with the ball attempts to connect three passes on one side of the grid, and then another three passes on the other side of the grid. If the ball goes out of bounds or the other team wins possession, then the roles change and the team that gains possession tries to connect three passes in each side of the grid. A point is earned by connecting three passes on one side of the grid and then moving the ball to the other side of the grid. Once a point is earned, the team with possession should maintain possession and try to get three passes in the other grid, thus earning another point.

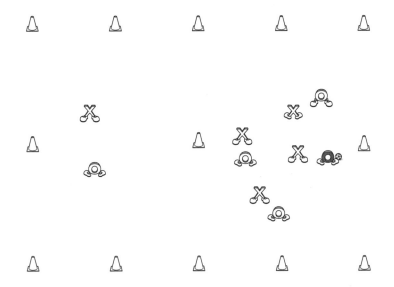

MODIFICATIONS
Adjust the number of passes required to earn a point. Add a third area between the scoring areas to give the teams an area of transition.

Drill 9 Corners

Team training

EQUIPMENT
1 ball; cones to set up a large grid and goals at each corner; pinnies

PLAYING AREA
Large grid 30 × 30 yards (27 × 27 m) up to half a soccer field, with a 5- × 5-yard (5 × 5 m) square in each corner of the grid (these squares are the goals)

PURPOSE
Teaching accurate passing and receiving, moving with and without the ball, communicating, and playing the ball in different directions

PROCEDURE
Divide players into two equal teams. Teams are each assigned two goals to score in on opposite corners (diagonally) of the grid. A goal is scored when players successfully pass the ball into one of their goals and a teammate stops the ball in the scoring square. They must pass the ball into the goal; it cannot be dribbled into the square. After a goal is scored, the other team gets possession of the ball starting outside the goal that was just scored in. Only one player from the team trying to score is allowed into the scoring square at a time. Defenders are not allowed to go into the opponent's goals.

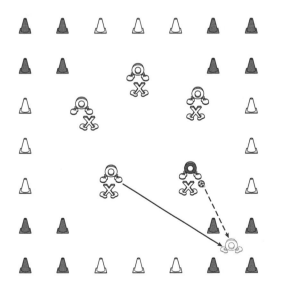

Drill 10 Half In, Half Out

Team training

EQUIPMENT
1 ball; cones to make a grid; pinnies

PLAYING AREA
Square grid 15 × 15 yards to 40 × 40 yards (14 × 14 m to 37 × 37 m) depending on number of players

PURPOSE
Teaching accurate passing and receiving, moving with and without the ball, and communicating

PROCEDURE
Divide players into two equal teams. Half the members of each team spread out around the outside of the grid while the remaining players from each team try to maintain possession of the ball inside the grid. Players on the outside can be used as support for their teammates on the inside. For example, a red player inside the grid can pass to another red teammate inside the grid or to a red teammate at the outside edge of the grid. The players around the outside should be encouraged to quickly find a teammate inside to pass the ball to. Play for several minutes, then switch the players on the inside and outside of the grid.

MODIFICATIONS
Restrict the players on the outside to one-touch passing only. Allow the players on the outside to pass to another player on the outside. Have the players on the outside come into the grid when they receive a ball; the inside players who passed the ball would then go to the outside and take their place along the side of the grid. Allow the teams to earn points for a certain number of consecutive passes.

The Coach's Clipboard

✔ Passing should be done with a purpose.

✔ Do not let your players learn to pass with the toes.

✔ Give players passing take-home challenges. Encourage them to use a wall if they do not have someone to pass to at home.

✔ The three factors that determine the purpose of a pass are power, accuracy, and timing.

✔ The inside-of-the-foot pass is the most fundamental pass. Emphasize this pass in particular.

✔ Instruct players to swing the leg from the hip, rather than just from the knee, when they are passing.

✔ When in the defensive half of the field, players should be safe with their passes; on the offensive side, they can take chances to create scoring opportunities.

✔ Remind players to always expect to get the ball and to communicate about who is available to receive a pass and where the defenders are located.

✔ When receiving a pass, players should cushion the ball like an egg or water balloon as it arrives.

✔ Encourage players to receive with the thigh or chest if the ball is off the ground. Discourage the use of the shin, abdomen, or face.

Teaching Shooting Skills With 10 Simple Drills

GOOOAAAL! In golf, it's a 300-yard drive right down the middle of the fairway; in baseball, a home run. It might be a strike in bowling, a diving catch in the end zone, or a three-pointer—nothing but net. In every sport there is a special feeling that comes when perfect execution meets perfect timing. In soccer, that feeling comes from driving the ball past the goalkeeper into the back of the net. It's raising your arms in triumph as you turn to see your teammates jumping into the air; it's hearing the parents erupt as if they're at the Olympic Games.

Scoring a goal in a soccer game can be a thrilling, emotional, even spiritual event. Maybe it's because so few goals are scored in a typical soccer game. Whatever the reason, there is a euphoric sense of triumph that comes with a great goal, and that euphoria is downright addictive. As a coach, this is something to take great advantage of, because players enjoy practicing shooting. It is fun, feedback is immediate, and the results are obvious. However, the reality is that few players in the United States have mastered the art of goal scoring. Players need help in consistently shooting with the proper technique and developing an attacking mentality. This is where you come in, Coach!

Designing a Shooting Practice

You won't need a motivational speech to keep players going during a shooting practice. However, to make sure a shooting practice is as much fun for spectators as it is for your players, be sure not to let anyone park a car behind or near the goal!

Although shooting may be incorporated into other practices, in a practice devoted to shooting alone, players can focus on getting creative, being selfish, and scoring goals almost the entire time. A shooting practice gives players *lots* of shooting technique repetition and opportunities to practice shooting in various situations. As shown in figure 5.1, you can follow the standard five-part practice format, focusing on technique at the beginning of the practice and emphasizing game scenarios toward the end of practice.

Keep in mind that shooting requires explosive muscle movements, so a good warm-up is important. You'll also want to have plenty of soccer balls to minimize time spent shagging balls and waiting in line. The following tips will help you conduct an effective shooting practice:

- Make shooting drills similar to game situations.
- Have all players practice one-versus-one attacking.
- Encourage players to be creative, take chances, and try new things.
- Use a goalkeeper, if your age group plays with them, in shooting drills.
- Practice shooting in all types of situations.
- Practice shooting with both feet.

Inspiring your players during a shooting practice will be like trying to get them excited about an amusement park. Many of them will be more interested and enthusiastic than you've seen them all season long. The challenge is getting them to focus on proper technique. One approach is to break down the technique into the smallest specific details. You can take your players through a progressive routine to help them put all the pieces together. Begin focusing on just one aspect and then add each detail, one at a time.

First, have your players lie on their bellies with a ball under one of their feet. They should lock the ankle, with the toes pointed down, and strike down on the top of the ball. Tell them to swing from the hip, so the entire leg is coming off the ground, rather than snap at the knee. This mirrors the actual movement they would use if they were standing over a ball shooting, but the focus now is on how it feels to properly strike the ball. Have them strike the ball with the right foot and the left foot. You can

Figure 5.1 Sample Shooting Practice Plan

Coach: _____ Date: _____

Time: _____

Age group: <u>Any</u>   Theme: <u>Shooting</u>

Practice part	Duration	Equipment	Activity or drill
Skill warm-up	5-10 min.	1 ball for every 2 players	*Jog and shoot:* Players jog across the field and back, passing a ball with a partner. When the pairs get back to the original sideline, one stands on the line and the other faces him, about 5-10 yards away. Players use proper shooting technique to play the ball back and forth. Then have the partners move close to one another. One player picks up the ball and serves it to the partner just below knee height. The kicking partner uses proper shooting technique to return the ball. After 10 touches with each foot, roles change. Stretch when finished.
Skill training	10 min.	Several balls, 1 cone, 1 goal	*Check, pass, shoot* (see page 107)
Water break			
Team training	10-15 min.	Several balls, pinnies, 2 cone goals, cones for boundaries	*Numbers* (see page 114)
Water break			
Games	10-15 min.	1 ball (plus extras), pinnies, 2 goals (real or cones), cones for field boundaries	*Dog owns the yard* (see page 116)
Cool-down	5 min.	None	*Shadow shooting:* Players line up along the sideline and jog across the field and back. Then they repeat the jog, going through the motions for taking a shot every few steps with both the right foot and the left. *Stretch* when finished.

From L. Blom and T. Blom, 2009, *Survival Guide for Coaching Youth Soccer* (Champaign, IL: Human Kinetics).

even have the players close their eyes so all they are concentrating on is the feeling of properly striking the ball.

Next, have the players lie on their backs with a partner standing at their feet, holding a ball just above their shoes. Again, focusing on proper form, the player lying on the ground raises one leg and strikes the middle of the ball. (The ball should stay in the partner's hands). Players should be moving the leg from the hip, with the knee bent slightly and the ankle locked, toes pointed down. The standing partner shouldn't be able to see the bottom of the partner's shoe.

After both players have completed several repetitions with the right and left foot, continue in the same position, but have the standing player drop the ball down toward the teammate's foot. The player on the ground should strike the ball back up into the partner's hands. You can easily identify poor technique and ankles that are not staying locked if the soccer ball does not go straight back up to the partner.

Once the players are consistently striking the ball, have both players stand facing one another. One player leans over, with the ball in his hands at about the height of his shin. Focusing on proper technique, the player strikes the ball out of his own hands, shooting it to his teammate, who sends it back the same way. Now, along with the physical positioning, players are focusing on following through after the kick. After kicking the ball out of their own hands, they should follow through and land forward on the shooting foot.

Continue the progression with the ball on the ground and players shooting back and forth. The focus for all these exercises should be proper technique rather than power. This progression should lead into shooting drills where players can do repetitions without worrying about defenders or other factors that might distract from proper form.

Shooting Technique

Shooting is really just passing the ball into the goal. In other words, the two main shooting techniques are similar to the inside-of-the-foot pass and the driven pass. Although a goal is a goal, at an early age, promoting correct technique is crucial. At U6, Quick Katie may be able to score with her toe, but as she begins to play at a more competitive level, this technique will not work as well. So, as you have heard before—*no toes*! Remind your players of this.

Inside-of-the-Foot Shot   The inside-of-the-foot shot is the most accurate scoring option and can be used to put the ball in a particular place in the goal. This is essentially an inside-of-the-foot pass (see chapter 4)

that is directed at the goal. It has a different purpose but involves the same technique. Players use this type of shot in the following situations: They are within a few yards of the goal, so power is not necessary to reach the goal; part of the goal is open, thereby dictating where the shot should go; or they have the strength to put enough power on a shot with the inside of the foot from where they are on the field. The inside of the foot is not used as often to shoot as the top of the foot is used.

Driven Shot

The driven shot is the most common shot and is used when players want power behind their strike. Powerful shots are hard for goalkeepers to handle and are necessary when a player is shooting at a distance. The mechanics are similar to the driven pass because contact is made with the top of the foot (the laces). The fundamental difference is in the follow-through. To keep the ball from skyrocketing over the goal, players need to lean over the ball and land on the kicking foot upon completion of the shot. As with passing (see page 70), practicing without shoes and socks can be helpful at first.

The approach to this shot is important. Because power is key, players cannot correctly drive the ball if they are in a stationary position before making contact. Players should use a three-step approach, starting with a step from the nonkicking foot. They should keep the ball between them and the target, with their hips facing the target. Both knees should be bent slightly. Because the goal does not move, unlike when passing to a human target, players should keep their eyes on the ball. The crowd will let them know if they scored.

As the nonkicking foot is planted about 4 to 6 inches (10 to 15 cm) to the side of the middle of the ball, the player should take a backswing from the hip with the kicking leg. On the kicking leg, the player should lock the ankle and point the toe down toward the ground. The toe should just scrape the grass as the laces of the shoe strike the middle of the ball (see figure 5.2). The player should lean over the ball, keeping the head, shoulders, and knees over the ball as he strikes through it. You can even use the song "Head, Shoulders, Knees, and Toes" to remind players to keep their bodies over the ball, but in this case it's head, shoulders, knees, *no toes*.

Figure 5.2   On a driven shot, the player keeps his eyes on the ball. During the kick, the ankle is locked, with the toe pointing down, so that the toe scrapes the grass as the laces strike the middle of the ball.

Players should contact the middle to top half of the ball—in order to keep the shot low—and follow through after striking the ball, landing on the kicking foot. By landing on the kicking foot, players stay facing the target, upright and balanced. A lack of balance will send the shot off target.

Shooting Angles

There is a certain amount of strategy to be employed when in front of the other team's goal. Getting in position to take a shot is the obvious objective. However, the real key to success is not to just take any old shot; you want your players to take a *good* shot. Don't panic, the difference is a subtle one. You won't need to create an algorithm for this, and your 7-year-olds don't need high school geometry. We are, however, going to challenge you with a little word problem:

> Player 1 is preparing to shoot. She is in the center of the field about 10 yards (9 m) out from the goal (see figure 5.3a). Player 2 is screaming for the ball because she is open and wants to score. That player is only 8 yards (7 m) out from the goal but is off center toward the sideline (see figure 5.3b). Assuming all other variables are equal and the goalkeeper will move to face the shooter, which player actually has the better chance of scoring?

The answer is that player 1 has the better chance of scoring because she has a better angle of opportunity (more open space). So the lesson learned is that players in the center of the field have the best opportunity

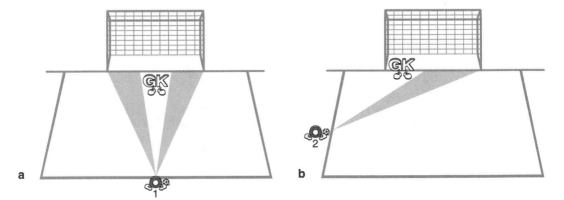

Figure 5.3   (*a*) Player 1 in the center of the field has a better angle to score than (*b*) player 2, who is positioned near the sideline.

Garbage Goals

After a shot is taken, players should follow the shot in case it bounces off an opponent, the goalkeeper, the goalpost, or a teammate. An offensive rebound in front of the goal could easily set up a second opportunity to score. Such opportunities typically go to players who remain active after the initial shot and work hard to get into position. Coach your players to expect the ball to come back out to them. If they believe it is going to hit a post or the goalkeeper is going to drop the ball, then they will be ready when it actually happens.

When following a shot, players do not need to worry about technique. The only objective at this point is to provide a surface of the body to make contact with the ball in order to redirect it toward the goal. We call these goals garbage goals because they don't typically come from a beautiful buildup or flawless technique; they come from hard, dirty work. However, the result is the same—a point on the scoreboard.

to score. Now if the goalkeeper is picking dandelions that are by the right side of the goal, then there is no problem attacking toward the left side. Assuming that the goalkeeper is in the correct position because his coach has also read this book, then it is important to get the ball back into the middle of the field for the best scoring opportunity.

Another way to increase the chance of scoring is by shooting low. The low shots may not show up on the highlight reel on *SportsCenter*, but the majority of all goals scored in soccer are within 3 feet (1 m) of the ground. Bicycle kicks, diving headers, and shots bent into the upper corner are all exciting, but they don't happen nearly as often as a well-placed shot into the bottom corners of the goal. One of the biggest benefits of taking a low shot is that even a poorly struck ball can turn out okay. If a player is trying to hit a shot high into the goal, the margin for error is small. If the ball is just a little too high, then it goes out of bounds and the other team gains possession.

Developing an Offensive Mentality

As a coach, you will soon learn that there is more to scoring goals than just using the correct technique. Players must learn how to attack! Attacking is a mentality that involves confidence and risk taking, and players who have these personality traits are often more successful in the offensive half of the field than are their peers. The mentality that young players need to develop in this half of the field is *go to the goal*. Tell your players to keep their eyes on the prize. Their goal *is* the goal, and they should always be looking for ways to get the ball there. When in shooting range, players should ask themselves the following questions:

- Can I score?
- Can I help my teammate score?
- Can we keep possession of the ball?

These questions have a hierarchy. The main mission, should the players choose to accept it, is to get that ball into the back of the net. If they are in a position to get the job done, then that is what they are to do. If they can't do it themselves, they should be looking and listening for a teammate who is in a position to score. Finally, if they really can't create a good scoring opportunity at that time, the focus should be on maintaining possession of the ball. It is important that you include this in your coaching tips. Once they are all pumped up to get a goal, they might start forcing shots or taking shots that they aren't ready to take. It is better in those circumstances to just hold on to the ball and work as a team to create an opening to the goal.

Inevitably, goal scorers get the glory, and that glory feels really good. Teammates high-fiving, parents cheering, individual stats piling up, groupies and paparazzi fighting to get closer. So, it should be no surprise that sometimes kids get a little selfish when the opportunity to score presents itself. There is a fine line between being a selfish player and simply trying to be a great goal scorer. However, if you preach, "Pass, pass, pass, share the ball," then you will have players forcing passes and giving up good scoring chances. You need to give players the freedom and encouragement to be creative, take players on, take chances in the offensive end of the field, and be a little selfish when they have an opportunity to score.

Awareness and communication are the biggest assets for keeping the attacking mentality from taking a negative turn. Talk to your players about when and where on the field to take chances, and remind them that it takes more than just one person to create a goal. Scoring a goal is an accomplishment for the team, not just the last player to touch the ball. Praise players for assists as well as for goals. Communicate with parents about your philosophy for goal scoring so they don't have to make assumptions and conjectures. Finally, substitute and position your players so they all have an opportunity to score at some point each season. Some players will take to the goal-scoring mentality more than others, and those differences will help them as they continue to grow and develop. It is important to give creative attacking players the opportunity to flourish as long as it doesn't take away from the experience their teammates are having.

Crumbs of Wisdom

We once saw a coach bring a box of cookies to practice to create an analogy for scoring goals and keeping possession of the ball. He gave one cookie to one of his players, and of course, the player ate the cookie. He gave that same player another cookie but told him he wasn't allowed to eat it. The player handed it to one of his teammates who, in turn, ate the cookie. Then, the coach gave the entire box to the player and told him he couldn't eat any cookies right now and neither could any of his teammates. Right on cue, the player carried the box of cookies over to his bag and hid them away. When the player returned to the group, the coach asked him why he didn't bring them to one of the other teams practicing nearby. The obvious response followed: "Those are our cookies, Coach. We'll eat them later." Even the youngest players there could make the connection between scoring and cookies.

Attacking as a Team

The team's goal when attacking is to create a goal-scoring opportunity. To do this, players must attack the open space and get players forward. The main objective is to get into the open space behind the defenders and create open lanes to the goal. The open space may very likely be on the outside of the field. However, as we mentioned earlier, the scoring angle is not as good from the side of the goal as it is in the center of the goal. Defenders are taught to push the attackers wide. If attackers are pushed wide, they can stay wide to maintain possession of the ball, but they should bring the ball back into the center of the field with a cross or driven pass as they approach the goal.

The second part of attacking is to get players forward so the team can attack with numbers up. This means there are more offensive players attacking the goal than there are opponents (defenders) to guard the goal, giving the offense a better opportunity to score. To get numbers up on offense, players can attack the goal quickly before the defenders have time to get into position, or they can send extra players into the attacking half to help create scoring opportunities.

The following tips for your players can also increase your team's chances of scoring:

- Shoot early at the first chance to effectively hit the target.
- Shoot often.
- Be willing to shoot. Take the risk. You can't score if you don't shoot.

- Learn the correct technique, and practice, practice, practice.
- Aim low.
- Aim at the far post.
- Follow the shot (that is, move in toward the goal after the shot).
- Work together to attack the goal.
- Take on the defender one versus one.
- Attack quickly.

Drill 1 Ping-Ping

Skill warm-up, skill training

EQUIPMENT
1 ball and 6 cones for every 2 players

PLAYING AREA
Each pair needs a rectangular area 5 to 10 yards (5 to 9 m) wide and 10 to 30 yards (9 to 27 m) long. The length of the area should increase with age and ability. Use four cones to mark off the rectangular area, and use two to create a goal in the middle of the rectangle.

PURPOSE
Teaching proper shooting technique without pressure

PROCEDURE
Players should be paired up, with one player positioned at each end of the rectangular area. The player with the ball shoots on the cone goal, and the other player receives the ball on the other end of the grid. The player who receives the ball controls it and shoots it back across the grid.

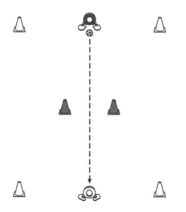

COACHING POINTS
Watch to make sure players are using correct technique and are focusing on accuracy more than on power. The ball should stay on or close to the ground on all shots.

MODIFICATIONS
Require players to use exactly two touches; the first controls the ball and the second is the shot. Put a player in the goal to challenge the shooters. Put two players on each end of the grid; one player controls the ball and sets up the other for the shot.

Drill 2 Space Invaders

Skill warm-up, skill training

EQUIPMENT
1 ball for every player; 8 cones; 1 goal

PLAYING AREA
15 to 30 yards (14 to 27 m) of field in front of the goal

PURPOSE
Teaching proper shooting technique through repetition

PROCEDURE
For level one, the players line up with balls 2 to 5 yards (2 to 5 m) in front of the goal. One at a time, each player shoots the ball into the goal, focusing on proper technique. Stand in or behind the goal so you can see their feet and judge their form. All the players who score using correct technique get to back up 3 to 5 yards (3 to 5 m) and try again from that distance; this is level two. Each successful attempt

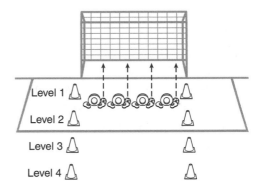

earns a player the opportunity to back up and try from farther away. Players who aren't successful stay at the original line and try again. To prevent players from getting blasted by shots of players at higher levels, let the players at the lowest level take their shots before letting the players at the next level go.

COACHING POINTS
The distance from the goal to the starting line and each subsequent line depends on the age and skill of the players. Older, stronger players can move farther from the goal each time. You can have four to six levels.

MODIFICATIONS
Require players to use the right foot and the left in order to move farther back. Have the players roll the ball in front of them slightly so they are striking a moving ball, as they would in most game situations. Require the shots to hit the net without the ball hitting the ground first.

Drill 3 Check, Pass, Shoot

Skill training, pregame warm-up

EQUIPMENT
Several balls; 1 cone; 1 goal

PLAYING AREA
20 to 30 yards (18 to 27 m) of field in front of the goal

PURPOSE
Teaching how to use proper shooting technique while in motion, check to open up for a teammate's pass, work with a teammate when attacking the goal, and follow the shot

PROCEDURE
Players line up (each with a ball) behind a cone out in front of the goal. Player 1, who has no ball, lines up between the goal and the line of players. Player 1 simulates breaking away from an imaginary defender by checking away from the first player in line (Player 2) and quickly checking back toward Player 2. As he 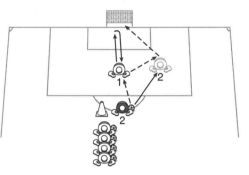 checks back toward Player 2, Player 1 calls for the ball and receives a pass. After passing the ball, Player 2 runs to the right or left of Player 1. Player 1 plays a short pass, leading Player 2 toward the goal. Player 2 shoots the ball on the first touch. Player 1 follows the shot, shags the ball after the play, and moves to the back of the line. Player 2 takes Player 1's position, and the drill begins again with the next player in line. If your age group plays with goalkeepers, place a player in goal for this drill.

COACHING POINTS
Emphasize communication between players. Encourage them to use changes of speed and direction to create space when checking to the ball. Remind them to pass the ball slightly in front of the shooter (not behind the shooter or too far in front) with the set-up pass.

MODIFICATIONS
Change the sequence so Player 1 turns with the ball (instead of passing it) and shoots.

Drill 4 Power-Finesse

Skill training, fun competition

EQUIPMENT
Several balls; 2 cones; 1 goal

PLAYING AREA
10 to 30 yards (9 to 27 m) of field in front of the goal

PURPOSE
Teaching players to take close shots and shots from a distance with one touch

PROCEDURE
Divide the players into two even teams; each team lines up behind a cone about 2 yards (2 m) outside the penalty box. On your command, the first player from one team moves toward the goal, and you serve a ball to the top of the penalty box from the goal. The player shoots the ball and continues toward the goal. You then serve a ball only a few yards from the goal, and the player shoots that ball.

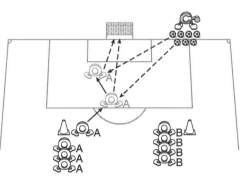

If the player fails to score with either shot, she is eliminated. If the player scores one goal, she moves to the back of her team's line. If the player scores both goals, she returns to her team's line and has the option of challenging any player from the other team. The player who is challenged takes a turn and must score both shots to avoid elimination. If the challenged player does score both shots, the challenger is eliminated. The first player from the second team now takes a turn. Play continues back and forth until all players from one team are eliminated.

COACHING POINTS
When players shoot from a distance, have them shoot on the first or second touch using the driven shot and tell them to focus on power. When they shoot close to the goal, have them shoot on the first touch using the inside-of-the-foot shot and tell them to focus on accuracy (finesse).

MODIFICATIONS
To limit the time, play to a certain score or for a set period of time rather than eliminating players. Add a goalkeeper (played by you or a helpful parent).

Drill 5 Everybody Keeps

Skill training, fun competition

EQUIPMENT
Several balls; 3 cones; 1 goal

PLAYING AREA
20 yards (18 m) of field in front of the goal

PURPOSE
Teaching proper shooting technique for medium-range shots taken with the first touch

PROCEDURE
Divide the players into two equal teams. Teams line up at a cone on either side of the goal with approximately 1 yard (1 m) between the post and each cone. Designate one team as shooters and the other as keepers. Stand at a cone with all the balls 12 to 20 yards (11 to 18 m) out from the center of the goal. On your command, the first shooter sprints onto the field, runs around you, and shoots a ball served by you. The shot

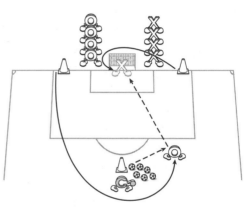

should be taken on the first or second touch. At the same time, the first keeper runs around behind the goal and then becomes the goalkeeper and tries to stop the shooter's shot. As soon as the shot is taken, the next shooter and keeper start their runs. The shooters get a point for every goal scored during their turns. Play continues 1 to 2 minutes, and then the teams switch places and roles.

COACHING POINTS
After each team has shot from the same side, change directions of the runs so players practice shooting with the other foot.

MODIFICATIONS
With more advanced players, make the services more challenging by bouncing them or playing them wider away from the goal.

Drill 6 Money Ball

Skill training, team training, fun competition

EQUIPMENT
Several balls; 4 cones; 1 goal

PLAYING AREA
Use cones to mark the start of two lines 10 to 25 yards (9 to 23 m) in front of the goal. Create a gate by placing two cones 5 to 10 yards (5 to 9 m) apart (wide for younger players, narrow for older players), parallel to the goal and halfway between the goal and the start of the lines.

PURPOSE
Teaching players to use proper shooting technique and to play quality passes to set up shots for teammates

PROCEDURE
Divide the players into two equal teams: team A and team B. Half the players from each team line up behind one of the cones that are 10 to 25 yards (9 to 23 m) from the goal. The other half of each team line up next to the opposite goalpost. Teams are diagonal from their teammates. The players in the lines next to the goal need soccer balls. Choose a ball that looks different from the others, and designate it the money ball. The first player from team A's line next to the goal stands in the goal. The first player from team B's line next to the goal passes a ball through the gate toward team B's line on the field and then runs around the playing area to the back of that line. As soon as the pass is made, the first player from team B's line on the field runs to the ball and shoots it. After the shot, the shooter (from team B) becomes the goalkeeper, and the goalkeeper (from team A) goes to the back of team A's line next to the goal.

The drill continues by having the first player from team A's line next to the goal pass a ball through the gate to team A's line on the field. The drill goes back and forth between teams with the following rotation: shooter, goalkeeper, back of the passing line. Award one point for every goal scored and *three* points for a goal scored with the money ball. If a pass does not go through the gate, that shot is forfeited and the shooter immediately becomes the goalkeeper. Play continues for a set period of time or until a specified score is reached. Teams are responsible for keeping balls available in their passing line, so players in line should shag balls while waiting for their turn. When the money ball is shot, it is up for grabs by anyone.

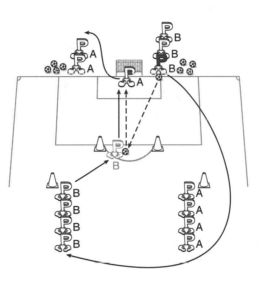

COACHING POINTS

Instruct players to give good passes to help set up their teammates to score. Remind players to work hard, stay alert, and communicate to help teammates remember the rotation and gain control of the money ball. Have teams switch sides so players are required to shoot with both the right foot and the left.

MODIFICATIONS

Consider subtracting a point for shots that are way off target to encourage players to focus on quality execution.

Drill 7 Battle Ball

Skill training, team training, fun competition

EQUIPMENT
1 ball for every player and extras; 4 cones; 2 goals

PLAYING AREA
Two goals facing each other 15 to 35 yards (14 to 32 m) apart; cones should be used to create a 4- × 4-yard (4 × 4 m) square halfway between the goals

PURPOSE
Teaching players to shoot a ball that is moving and apply proper technique for medium-range shots

PROCEDURE
Divide players into two equal teams; one team lines up next to each goal. The first player from team A stands in his own goal. On your command, the first player on team B passes the ball into the square, then follows his pass and shoots the ball from within the square. The team A player in the goal attempts to stop the shot. As soon as the shot is taken, the team B shooter backs up into his team's goal and becomes a goalkeeper. The goalkeeper from team A goes to the back of his team's line. Then the process is repeated as the next player in line for team A passes a ball into the square, follows it, shoots, and then backs up to become a goalkeeper. If any shooter's ball leaves the square, the shooter forfeits that shot and immediately becomes a goalkeeper. Award one point for each goal scored.

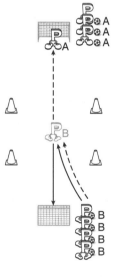

COACHING POINTS
Instruct players to play an accurate, well-paced pass into the box to set up the shot. Instruct shooters to look for advantages created by goalkeepers who are out of position or slow to get back in front of the goal.

MODIFICATIONS
Have the players toss the ball into the square so they are required to follow and shoot a bouncing ball. Consider playing the ball into the square yourself instead of having the players do it.

Drill 8 World Cup

Team training, fun competition

EQUIPMENT
Several balls; 1 goal

PLAYING AREA
Area in front of the goal; 20 yards (18 m) up to the entire half field

PURPOSE
Teaching players to work together as a team to score, shoot in unpredictable situations, and follow shots

PROCEDURE
Pair up players, or put them in teams of three. Each team chooses a country to represent. Assign a player, an assistant coach, or a parent to be the goalkeeper. Teams position themselves in front of the goal; all the teams play at the same time. You serve a ball randomly into the space, and teams work against one another to score. When a ball goes into the goal or out of play, send in another ball, attempting to keep play continuous. When a team scores, those players leave the field, slowly decreasing the number of teams left on the field. The final team left on the field is eliminated from the drill, and the teams who scored go back onto the field and play again. One team is eliminated each round until there is a World Cup champion.

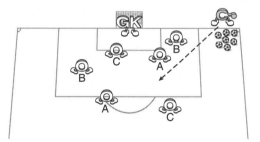

COACHING POINTS
Encourage players to work as a team, communicate with teammates, use proper shooting technique, and follow the shots. You can have the players from eliminated teams shag and serve balls.

MODIFICATIONS
Send in more than one ball at a time, but consider having a coach in goal rather than a player if you are going to do this. Restrict how players can score (such as left foot only, first touch).

Drill 9 Numbers

Team training, fun competition

EQUIPMENT
Several balls; 8 to 12 cones to set up goals and boundaries for the field; pinnies

PLAYING AREA
Set up two goals facing each other 10 to 30 yards (9 to 27 m) apart. You can use cones placed 2 to 5 yards (2 to 5 m) apart or real goals. If you use real goals, include a goalkeeper. Set up cones to mark the sidelines about 10 to 20 yards (9 to 18 m) from each other.

PURPOSE
Teaching players how to create scoring opportunities, keep the ball low with their shots, become comfortable taking on players 1v1, and attack in small groups

PROCEDURE
Divide the players into two equal teams. Teams line up on opposite sidelines. If your team plays with goalkeepers and the space is adequate, place a goalkeeper in each goal. Each team is assigned a goal to score into. Players on each team should be numbered so each player has a counterpart on the other team. (If the teams aren't even, one player could be assigned two numbers.) Serve a ball onto the field and call a number. The players assigned that number enter the field and try to score. Once a goal is scored, those players return to their lines, and you send a new ball onto the field and call a new number.

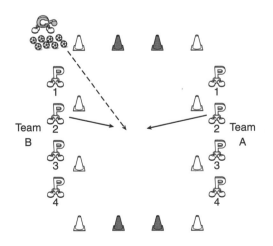

COACHING POINTS

Encourage players to move quickly to the ball to gain possession, be creative with attacking moves, create space for shots by changing speed and direction, and attack the opponent's front foot (to catch the defender off guard or to force her to turn so the dribbler can get the ball past her).

MODIFICATIONS

Call more than one number at a time. You can also allow players on the sidelines to kick the ball back into play if it comes near them to assist the players in the middle.

Drill 10 Dog Owns the Yard

Team training, games, fun competition

EQUIPMENT
1 ball; cones to set up field boundaries; 2 goals; pinnies

PLAYING AREA
Two goals facing each other 10 to 40 yards (9 to 37 m) apart (distance increases with age, ability, and the number of players); width of playing area is 10 to 30 yards (9 to 27 m) (the field should be longer than it is wide)

PURPOSE
Teaching players to attack as a team in gamelike situations

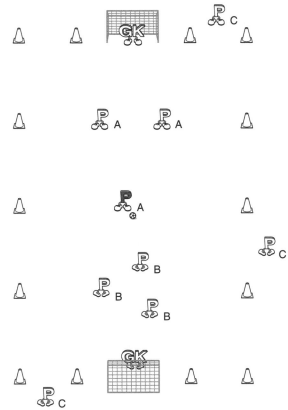

PROCEDURE
Divide the players into three or more teams of equal number. The smaller the teams, the more touches and shooting opportunities players will have. Two teams start on the field, and the other teams help shag balls and stay ready for their opportunity to play. The teams on the field scrimmage. The first team to score wins. The winning team stays on the field; the losing team is quickly replaced by one of the resting teams. The team that has been off the longest should rotate onto the field each time. If neither team scores within a set period of time, both teams are replaced. If you have only three teams, the team that has been on the field the longest remains on the field in the event of a tie. Using goalkeepers is optional, and it will decrease the number of times teams score.

COACHING POINTS
Encourage players to attack the center of the goal quickly as a team. To be successful, they will need to take shots quickly before their opponents have time to set up in defensive position.

The Coach's Clipboard

✔ Teach proper shooting technique in small parts so players learn each step correctly. Then practice shooting at game speed.

✔ Remind players to use the inside-of-the-foot shot when accuracy is more important than power.

✔ Remind players to use the driven (laces) shot when shooting for power or distance.

✔ When shooting, players should position themselves behind the ball so the hips are facing the goal and the plant foot is pointing toward the target.

✔ With a driven shot, players should keep their heads, shoulders, and knees over the top of the ball. When shooting, players should contact the middle to top half of the ball to keep the shot low.

✔ Instruct players to follow through the ball and land on the kicking foot.

✔ Tell players to follow the shot and be prepared for the ball to come back out to them after a shot. To score goals, players need an attacking mentality.

✔ Teach players when to shoot and when to pass.

✔ Players should attack the open space quickly before defenders have time to set up in the correct positions.

Teaching Defensive Skills With 10 Simple Drills

In a sport where most games are decided by one goal, limiting the number of goal-scoring opportunities for the other team is a worthwhile strategy. Sound defense requires practice, organization, teamwork, and communication. A good defender must be patient, confident, and persistent. Contrary to popular opinion, the defense is not always the best place to hide the less-talented members of your team. There is a great chance that your team won't have an abundance of strong, fast players fighting to play in the back, so you'll make due with what you've got. The key is to sell your players on the idea that playing good defense is just as important as taking players on and scoring goals. Then, help them develop an understanding of what it means to play defense.

For older players, defense is about pride; it's about outworking the opponent. It's about being determined not to let the opposition get the upper hand. For most of your kids, the idea is much simpler: *Stop that guy.* Really and truly, the role of the defense is to stop the other team from doing something dangerous, from creating a quality goal-scoring opportunity.

The key to coaching good defense is to overcome two obstacles. First, you must prevent all your players from hanging out in front of the goal your team is attacking. Kids want to score, and they want to chase the ball all over the field, but if your entire team goes forward, you'll be vulnerable to a counterattack. The second obstacle is that most of your players have never observed a high-level soccer game, let alone good defensive play. This is not to say that good defense is absent from soccer in your league, at the local college, or on television. Most spectators just aren't watching for that. It's easy to recognize passing, dribbling, and shooting, but kids usually do not watch and learn from the players without the ball. If you initially focus on overcoming these two pitfalls, defense will be relatively easy to incorporate into your team's playing style.

Designing a Defensive Practice

As important as defense can be to a team's success, it is often neglected in training. For whatever reason, coaches seem to spend more time working on offensive skills and strategies. Include a defensive practice early in the season so the players understand it is important. Figure 6.1 provides an example of a sample defending practice.

Praise and reinforce players who volunteer for or show an interest in playing defense. Their offensive teammates will get plenty of praise for beating players and scoring goals. And make sure the players understand that everyone is responsible for helping the team develop a solid defense. Every single player will have an opportunity to pressure the ball and support a teammate no matter what position he is playing.

Just as when teaching a technical skill such as dribbling or shooting, it is important to be clear and focused with your defensive practices. Most of your work should be based on the role of the first defender. Because many of the kids may have never paid close attention to defense, break the movements down to help them really see what good defense should look like. As you progress through each practice and add attackers and goals, stop the play occasionally to point out and praise players who are defending well.

Defense is about effort and attitude. You'll want and need your players to work hard as defenders, so help them get excited about the challenge. For most of the first few practice sessions with younger age groups, focus on correct individual defending. Once they understand individual defending, move to basic ideas of team defending, slowly adding attackers and defenders to your drills.

Figure 6.1 Sample Defending Practice Plan

Coach: _____   Date: _____

Time: _____

Age group: <u>Any</u>   Theme: <u>Individual defending</u>

Practice part	Duration	Equipment	Activity or drill
Skill warm-up	10-15 min.	1 ball for every 2 players	*First-defender warm-up* (see page 131) *Stretching*
Skill training	10 min.	1 ball per lane, 6-8 cones for boundaries of each lane	*Defensive driving lane* (see page 133)
Water break			
Team training	10-15 min.	Several balls, 1 cone, 1 goal	*1v1 to goal* (see page 134)
Water break			
Games	10-15 min.	1 ball, 2 goals, pinnies	*Shadow scrimmage* (see page 138)
Cool-down	5 min.	None	*Puppet master* (see page 129) *Stretch* when finished.

From L. Blom and T. Blom, 2009, *Survival Guide for Coaching Youth Soccer* (Champaign, IL: Human Kinetics).

Teaching Individual Defending

As the other team enters your defensive half of the field, you may experience increased nervousness, an upset stomach, or a racing heart. You are not alone; the parents on the sidelines and more importantly your defenders are probably feeling the same way. So you need to remain in control; resist the temptation to scream, "Get the ball!" or "Kick it out!" Although those behaviors may reduce the chance that the attackers will score this time down the field, it is difficult to be effective with this defensive approach over the course of an entire game.

The main goal for your defenders is to simply slow down the attacking team. The first defender (the first player to approach the player with the ball—usually the player who is closest to the attacker) is the first line of defense. This player needs to use proper defending technique to slow down the attacker and allow the rest of her team to get into good defensive position. The first defender should focus on four techniques to be successful: the approach, the defensive stance, the defensive hierarchy, and winning the ball. The first technique involves the best way to move to the attacker. Once the defender is close to the attacker, she then needs to get into correct defensive stance. While defending, players should think about the four priorities of defending, or the defensive hierarchy. And if the time is right, the defender may try to win the ball from the attacker.

Approaching the Attacker

The main job of the defensive player who becomes the first defender is to slow down the attack by not allowing the dribbling player to have free reign of the field. Encourage the first defender to step to the ball, which involves making a strong movement of several aggressive steps toward the player with the ball to put pressure on the attacker. Pressuring the attacker causes that player to slow down, delaying the attacking team.

When pressuring the ball as the first defender, players must learn how to correctly approach the attacker. Players should approach with speed to close down the space between them and the attacker, but as they get close to their opponent, they need to slow down. Your Speedy Gonzales on the team may be quick, but if he doesn't slow down well, he will end up running past the attacker, into the attacker, or over the attacker. None of those outcomes is very helpful.

Players should approach from the goal side of the attacker and from an angle that channels the attacker to the sideline of the field as shown in figure 6.2. If you were to draw a line from the attacker to the goal, the defender should be in that path. The attacker should

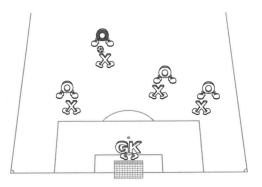

Figure 6.2 When a defender is goal side of the attacker, the defender is between the attacker and the goal.

not be able to get to the goal without going around the defender. When the attacker is within shooting range of the goal, the defender should lead him toward the sideline of the field and away from the goal. To do this, the defender should stand using a staggered stance angled open toward the sideline. Forcing the opponent to the sideline decreases the attacker's shooting angle.

Players should generally stand about a broomstick (1 yard; 1 m) away from an attacker. If the attacker is faster than the defender, the defender should allow for a little more room. If the defender is faster than the attacker, the defender can get a little closer. Tell your players that if they can smell the attacker's breath, they are too close. If the attacker has time to smile for the camera before feeling pressure, the defenders are too far away. Defensive players should typically get closer to the attacker as the attacker gets closer to the goal.

Using the Defensive Stance

Players should use a staggered stance when pressuring the attacker. One foot should be in front of the other about shoulder-width apart. Their hips will not be facing the attacker; they will be at a 45-degree angle to the attacker, open to the side of the field toward which they want their opponent to go. If they stand perpendicular (hips at a 90-degree angle to the attacker), the attacker can move behind them before they have time to turn. If the attacker gets in behind the defense, she has a better opportunity to score. She has fewer obstacles in the way of her goal. If a defender stands facing forward (hips are parallel, or flat, with the attacker), the attacker can easily run past because the defender cannot effectively stay in front of the attacker; the defender may even end up flat on her back.

The other result of standing flat is having the attacker knock the ball between the defender's legs, which is often referred to as a *nutmeg*. A nutmeg is generally accepted as the worst possible way to be beaten by an opponent because it means the attacker is so superior that he can just go right through the defender rather than having to go around. A nutmeg is the equivalent of throwing up an air ball in basketball or missing an extra point in football. Being nutmegged is no fun at all, trust us!

So for the perfect defensive stance (see figure 6.3), players should stand on the balls of their feet. (Standing flatfooted prevents them from being able to move quickly in response to an attacker's movement.) The knees should be bent slightly to give players a low center of gravity, which allows quick movement and change of direction. The chest should be slightly forward over the toes. Players cannot move as quickly if they are completely upright, and they will likely fall back if they are leaning backward.

Figure 6.3   Proper defensive stance.

Unfortunately the ball moves, so being in this perfect defensive stance will not last very long if the defender does not learn how to jockey and shuffle while pressuring the attacker. Jockeying means staying in the attacker's path (on the goal side) with a broomstick distance and proper defensive stance. The defender moves side to side and backward to stay in front of the attacker, working to slow her down.

Instruct your players to focus on the ball, not on the attacker's legs or feet, as they jockey. This is not as crucial at the younger age groups, but as the attackers become more experienced and learn moves, they will work to deceive the defenders. For a first defender, the most important cue is the ball. Forget the attacker. Let him dance around the ball all he wants. Don't let your players dive in to get the ball. Coach them to jockey attackers, staying in front of them and keeping them away from the goal.

To stay in front of the attacker, players need to be prepared to shuffle and backpedal. Players should maintain the correct defensive stance, with their feet shoulder-width apart and one foot in front of the other, allowing their feet to shuffle across the grass. Players should not cross their feet; this will result in slower movement or maybe even falling down. Jockeying and shuffling keep defenders from chasing the ball. Players may think that getting the ball is the most important goal (the defensive version of beehive soccer), but this is not an effective defensive strategy. Defenders end up chasing the attackers around the field and not preventing an attack. Encourage your players to stay in their defensive positions and be patient.

Establishing a Defensive Hierarchy

Because players tend to jump right in and go after the ball, you will need to remind them of their responsibilities on a regular basis. Bruce Brownlee, expert on coaching youth soccer, recommends using the following four cues to help players remember their goals as defenders.* If you are musically inclined, it may even be worth making them into a song.

1. **No get.** If the defender can step into the path of the ball to prevent it from getting to the attacker, then encourage her to do so. This action is hard to do, unless defenders are in correct defensive position before the ball is played to the attacker. It is ideal for defenders to not let the attackers get the ball.

2. **No turn.** If the attacker does get the ball but receives it with his back to the goal, the defender's objective is to prevent him from turning around and facing the goal. If he can't see the goal, it is very difficult to shoot. To prevent the attacker from turning, the defender must be very close to the attacker. He should be able to touch the attacker's back with his arm extended while maintaining an angled stance, with feet shoulder-width apart and knees bent. The defender should be able to see the ball and move with the attacker.

3. **No move.** If the attacker is able to turn to face the goal, the defender's job now is to prevent her from moving closer to the goal. The defender needs to stay in the attacker's path toward the goal. It is okay for the attacker to move from side to side, but the defender does not want the attacker to move forward down the field. The closer the attacker gets to the goal, the higher the shooting percentage.

4. **No shoot.** As the attacker gets close to the goal, the defender must stay between him and the goal in order to prevent a shot. When the attacker is within shooting range, the defender's main goal is to not let the attacker shoot. To prevent the shot, the defender should stay on the goal side of the attacker, be able to see the opponent and ball, and be aware of the distance to the goal.

Winning the Ball

Approaching the ball, remaining in correct defensive stance, and knowing the goals for defense are only part of the battle. Defenders must also maintain a strong, patient mental approach in their role. Teach your

*Adapted, by permission, from B. Brownlee, 2002, *Bruce Brownlee soccer coaching notes.* [Online]. Available: http://www.soccercoachingnotes.com/coaching/tactical/no-get-no-turn-no-move-no-shoot. html [January 5, 2009].

defenders to have controlled aggression. Although it may seem like an advantage to have Barry the Beast as your main defender, you will want to help him learn how to appropriately use his size, strength, and aggression. If he goes crazy, he will not only cause fouls that result in free kicks for the other team but also may hurt other players. Teach him to pressure the ball first and wait for the right time to tackle the ball.

Obviously, your defenders aren't just going to jockey and shuffle backward into their own goal. At some point, defenders need to try to win the ball. The key is to wait and watch for the right time to challenge. Although the first defender's main goal is to pressure, there are times when it is appropriate to tackle. As the first defender is jockeying and maintaining a little space between herself and the ball, she should be looking for one of these three opportunities to win the ball from the dribbling player:

- The attacker makes a bad touch or pushes the ball too far away from her.
- The attacker stops the ball.
- The attacker looks down and cannot see her teammates or the field.

Even the best players you face will take a bad touch or push the ball out a little too far. Stress to your players to be patient and wait for that moment. Another good opportunity to tackle is when the dribbling player is making a decision. When the dribbler stops the ball or looks down at the ball, she is likely trying to decide what to do next. For that split second, her focus is off of the defender, and she is vulnerable to a tackle.

When the opportunity to tackle occurs, the defender must step quickly to the ball. The defender should be upright or even leaning forward over the ball, rather than leaning back and reaching with only the foot. Using the inside of the foot (the part of the shoe where the logo is usually located), the defender will bring the leg inward toward the ball, contacting the middle of the ball. There may be some contact made with the upper part of the body, and that is okay. As long as the contact is simply a result of both players challenging for the ball, no harm is done. Neither player is allowed to use the hands to grab, push, pull, or hit the opponent.

At this point, several outcomes are possible. One, the ball may scoot away, out of reach, from both players. Two, the ball may stay close to the players without either player having complete possession. Three, the defensive player gains possession of the ball and is able to get around the attacker. Four, the attacker keeps possession and gets around the defender. When the initial tackle doesn't win clear possession of the ball, which happens frequently, the player who keeps working and keeps fighting for the ball comes out with it. Remind your players to be persistent. Furthermore, every defender will get beaten at some point, probably at least once a game. It will happen, so teach your defenders how to recover rather than pout or be embarrassed. They can make it up to their teammates by continuing to help them defend.

Although your players may ask about slide tackles, which is when a defender dives, legs first, at the ball, do *not* use them as a primary weapon of defense. They are overrated. Unless it is the last possible option, defenders shouldn't slide tackle because it leaves them on the ground where they are unable to help their teammates or recover the ball. A standing tackle should be used more often, but remember the number one goal of the first defender is to *pressure*, not *win*, the ball.

Teaching Team Defending

Bruce Brownlee says that team defense is a dance, so individual players need to learn the steps, and the team needs to stay in rhythm. We have already discussed the individual steps of the approach and the stance. Now the team must learn how to put those steps together. Team defending is a complex concept that is typically taught to players who are 10 years and older or to players who are advanced in skill development. It requires team coordination and patience. A fairly simple concept that you should start with goes along with what you teach about offense: Not everyone should move to the ball at the same time.

The player closest to the ball should be the first defender. This player takes on the responsibilities discussed so far in this chapter. The main job is to pressure the ball and the player with the ball. Everyone else should be looking for ways to help defend, namely marking a player that could be dangerous or helping to support the first defender. The teammate closest to the first defender is called the second defender. (See the pattern forming here?) This player's job is to support the first defender and provide *cover*. The second defender should try to move close enough to the play to be able to win a loose ball that might get by the first defender or to apply pressure to the opponent if the first defender gets beaten. At the same time, it is important that the second defender not completely leave an assigned mark.

The next closest player—that's right, the third defender—should help provide *balance*. This player must make sure there is still some shape to the defense and that not all of the focus is directly on the ball. The third defender should be prepared to become the second defender or to adjust and move into position if the ball is passed to someone else.

Quite possibly, the most important job for you as a coach is to carefully decide how much information your team can handle about the second and third defender. With younger, inexperienced players, simply guiding them to support one another without going into kamikaze attacks on the ball is a great start. Remind them that the area around the player with the ball is the most dangerous area, but the entire field and all the members of the other team must be accounted for.

Defensive Styles

There are two main methods of organizing the team's defense: man-to-man and zone. These concepts are likely more information than first-time players can grasp. For this group, the concern is having players so focused on where they are supposed to be defensively that they lose sight of the free-flowing nature that makes soccer unique from many other sports. As the players develop and mature, you'll want to spend more time deciding what type of defensive philosophy your team will employ and how strictly you coach that system.

Man-to-man is the easiest to explain and conceptualize, but that doesn't always mean it's the easiest to play. In this system, each player on your team is assigned a counterpart from the opposition. When the other team gets the ball, each player's main job is to mark that specific opponent. The key is to remind the players that they can't assume their teammates are all going to play perfect defense for the entire game. Even when marking man-to-man, players must be prepared to switch, cover for one another, and support their teammates. In a man-to-man marking system, all players from the opposition are accounted for. However, if a player is outmatched, that becomes a key weakness the other team may exploit.

In a zone defense, each player is responsible for an area of the field and the player or players who enter that area. When introducing this system, it is smart to have the zones overlapping (see figure 6.4) so the players see that they must be prepared to help a nearby teammate who has more than one person in his zone. In a zone defense, the team's shape stays fairly consistent. There would rarely be much open space unaccounted for. This type of defense requires solid organization and communication and can be vulnerable against teams that move the ball especially well. Regardless of the system you choose to utilize, frequently include the basic concepts in your practices.

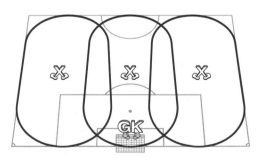

Figure 6.4 In a zone defense, assign each defender a zone (or vertical section) on the defensive side of the field. Zone areas should overlap slightly.

Drill 1 Puppet Master

Skill warm-up

EQUIPMENT
None

PLAYING AREA
Half the field or enough space for the players to line up side by side

PURPOSE
Teaching the proper defensive stance and proper movement in response to an attacker

PROCEDURE
Players line up across the sideline. Stand 10 to 15 yards (9 to 14 m) in front of the players. As you move forward, backward, and side to side, the players mirror the movement. So if you are backpedaling, the players are jogging forward.

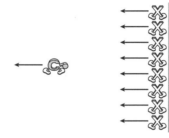

COACHING POINTS
Instruct your players to pay attention and react quickly to your movements. Some players may want to run past you; remind them to stay in front of you, as they would with an opponent.

MODIFICATIONS
Include jumping into the air, reaching down and touching the ground, skipping, and so on.

Drill 2 Shadow Defender

Skill warm-up, skill training

EQUIPMENT
1 ball for every 2 players

PLAYING AREA
Half the field or enough space for the players to line up side by side

PURPOSE
Teaching proper first-defender technique

PROCEDURE
Across the sideline, players line up facing a partner. The players facing the field slowly dribble toward their partners while the partners jockey backward, staying in front of the dribbling players and maintaining a constant space between them. When they reach the other side of the field, the players switch roles and go back across the field. Repeat several times, stressing the proper technique for the defenders. The speed and intensity of the dribblers' attack should increase each time they cross the field. After several opportunities to practice the proper stance and movement, allow the defenders to try to win the ball from the dribblers.

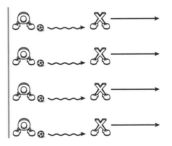

COACHING POINTS
Your players will want to go after the ball. Remind them to tackle the ball when it stops, when the dribbler takes a bad touch, or when the dribbler loses focus on the defender (looks down or looks around for an option).

Drill 3 First-Defender Warm-Up

Skill warm-up, skill training, pregame warm-up

EQUIPMENT
1 ball for every 2 players

PLAYING AREA
Half the field or large grid; enough cones to mark the area

PURPOSE
Teaching proper first-defender technique and movement

PROCEDURE
Make sure half your players each have a ball. All the players jog around within the field or grid; the players with a ball should dribble. On your command (use *pass*, *go*, or whatever word your players will understand), the players with a ball pass to players without a ball who are at least 7 yards (6 m) away. The player who passed the ball follows it and defends the player who received the ball, who dribbles at the defender for three or four steps. The players then go off in different directions, returning to jogging or dribbling until the next command. This continues for several minutes.

MODIFICATION
When players are comfortable with the basic moves, increase the difficulty by allowing the player who receives the ball to try to get past the defender and allowing the defender to work to win the ball.

Drill 4 Protect This House

Skill training, fun competition

EQUIPMENT
1 ball for every player; several small round cones (if available)

PLAYING AREA
Center circle or large area about half the size of the field

PURPOSE
Teaching proper defensive movement and positioning

PROCEDURE
Divide the players into three groups. Two groups dribble freely around the area, while the players in the third group work to protect their soccer balls. If you have round cones (disc cones), the players protecting balls should balance them on top of a cone. The protectors move around their own balls, defending them from the dribbling opponents. Those players dribbling around try to kick their balls into one of the balls being protected. Play for 1 to 2 minutes and then rotate the groups. Each time a protected ball gets hit or knocked off a cone, the player who was protecting the ball gets a strike. The goal is to get the least number of strikes.

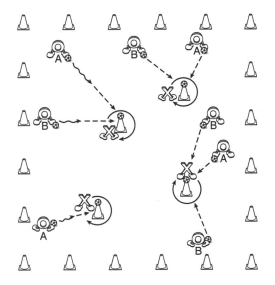

COACHING POINTS
Remind defenders to be ready to move quickly to stay in front of their balls as they look around at the attackers.

MODIFICATIONS
Rather than defending just their own balls, have all defenders work together to protect all the soccer balls.

Drill 5 Defensive Driving Lane

Skill training, team training

EQUIPMENT
1 ball per player; 6 to 8 cones for each lane

PLAYING AREA
Rectangular lanes 5 to 10 yards (4 to 9 m) wide and 10 to 15 yards (9 to 14 m) long (a narrow lane gives an advantage to a defender)

PURPOSE
Teaching the proper approach and stance of the first and second defenders and proper tackling technique

PROCEDURE
Divide the players into groups of 6 to 8. Each group works in its own lane. Within each lane, half the players go to each end, and all the balls are on one end. One player from each end of the grid steps into the lane. The player with the ball passes the ball down the lane to the other player. The player who receives the ball attempts to dribble past the player who passed the ball.

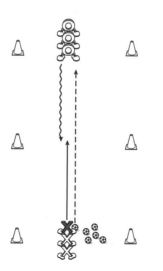

MODIFICATIONS
Add a second player from each end so they are playing 2v2.

Drill 6 1v1 to Goal

Skill training, team training, pregame warm-up

EQUIPMENT
Several balls; 1 cone; 1 goal

PLAYING AREA
Area in front of a goal out to midfield

PURPOSE
Teaching the proper approach and stance of the first and second defenders and proper tackling technique

PROCEDURE
Divide the players into two groups. One group lines up next to the goal, and the other group lines up at a cone near midfield. The players next to the goal have the soccer balls, and if your age group uses goalkeepers, a goalkeeper should be positioned in the goal. The first player next to the post kicks a ball out to the first player in the line on the field and then steps out to defend that player. The player who receives the ball attacks and tries to get past the defender to get a shot on goal. Players switch lines after each turn.

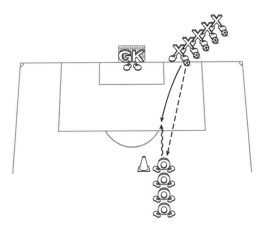

MODIFICATIONS
Add a second defender or add a second offensive player to force the defender to pressure the ball and stay aware of other attacking players.

Drill 7 Race to the Ball

Team training, pregame warm-up

EQUIPMENT
Several balls; 2 cones; 1 goal

PLAYING AREA
Area in front of a goal out to midfield

PURPOSE
Teaching the method for chasing down an opponent with the ball and getting into defensive position

PROCEDURE
Place all the balls at midfield. Players form two even lines at cones on either side of you. Serve a ball toward the goal, and give a command so that the first player from each line races to the ball. The first player to touch the ball is on offense and tries to score. The other player becomes the defender. The turn ends when the defender or goalkeeper gets possession of the ball or when the ball goes out of bounds.

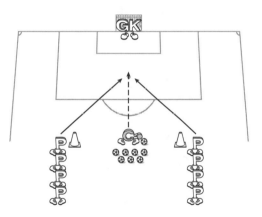

MODIFICATIONS
Serve the ball in the air; serve to one side to give one line an advantage; have the players sit, lie down, or turn their backs to the goal before you serve the ball.

Drill 8 Defend the Line

Team training

EQUIPMENT
1 ball; 6 to 10 cones to mark the playing area; pinnies

PLAYING AREA
Rectangular area 10 to 20 yards (9 to 18 m) wide and 10 to 15 yards (9 to 14 m) long (the field will actually be wider than long; the field should be wider for three or four defenders than for just two)

PURPOSE
Teaching team defending

PROCEDURE
Divide the players into groups of four, six, or eight depending on how many defenders you want working together. Each group is assigned to its own grid, and each group divides into two teams. Within the grid, the players on each team spread out so they are facing their opposition. The teams scrimmage within the grid, scoring a goal by carrying the ball across the opposite line. When on defense, players should work together to defend the entire line and cut off dribbling and passing lanes.

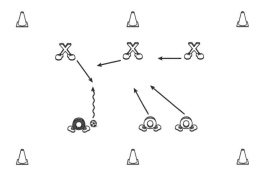

MODIFICATIONS
Allow players to earn a point for effectively defending as a team and preventing the attackers from scoring.

Drill 9 Turnover

Team training, games

EQUIPMENT
1 ball; 4 cones; 1 goal; pinnies

PLAYING AREA
Half a soccer field or a little less; use the cones to set up one small goal 2 to 4 yards (2 to 4 m) wide along each sideline, 20 to 40 yards (18 to 37 m) from the real goal

PURPOSE
Teaching team defense, moving from offense to defense, and attacking quickly after winning the ball on defense

PROCEDURE
A team of four defenders and one goalkeeper defends the real goal against three attackers. If the defensive unit wins possession of the ball, the players (excluding the goalkeeper) should try to score in one of the small goals positioned along the sideline. The team that was on offense switches to defense. Rotate extra players onto each team so everyone plays. The drill should run 10 to 15 minutes, switching players so everyone defends the large goal at some point.

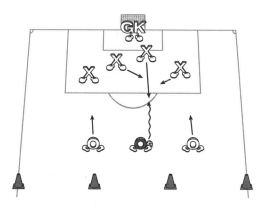

COACHING POINTS
Remind your players to work together and when they win the ball, to quickly become attackers. The other group must transition quickly into defenders after losing the ball.

MODIFICATIONS
Replace the "losing" team each time a goal is scored.

Drill 10 Shadow Scrimmage

EQUIPMENT
1 ball; 2 goals; pinnies

PLAYING AREA
Whole (7 v 7 or more players) or half (6 v 6 or fewer players) of the soccer field

PURPOSE
Teaching man-to-man team defending

PROCEDURE
Divide the players into two teams. If your age group use goalkeepers, put one in each goal. Each player is then paired with a member of the opposing team—this is his defensive mark for the entire scrimmage. Each player is allowed to defend only his specific counterpart on the other team. Players can go anywhere on the field, and they can fight for any loose ball. Once a player has possession of the ball, he can be challenged only by his counterpart.

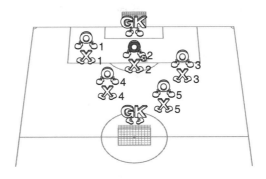

MODIFICATIONS
After a certain amount of time, allow another player to help defend the player with the ball.

The Coach's Clipboard

✔ Defense involves being patient and strong and out-working the attacker.

✔ The player closest to the ball should step to the ball and become the first defender.

✔ The first defender applies pressure to slow down the attack.

✔ The second defender covers any space left open by the first defender.

✔ The third defender balances the defense in case the attackers quickly switch the ball to the other side of the field.

✔ Teach the proper defensive stance: (1) staggered feet, (2) low center of gravity, (3) slight lean of trunk, and (4) standing on balls of feet.

✔ Encourage your defenders to jockey attackers, shuffling with and staying in front of them.

✔ Emphasize the goals for defenders: (1) Don't let attackers get the ball, (2) don't let them turn with the ball, (3) don't let them move toward the goal, (4) don't let them shoot on goal.

✔ Players should tackle when the attacker has a bad touch, stops the ball, or looks down.

Teaching Goalkeeping Skills With 10 Simple Drills

Long before your players get their driver's license or their first kiss, there is another rite of passage—playing soccer with goalkeepers. In most leagues, goalkeepers are introduced at U10, but check the guidelines specific to your league. You don't want to show up for the first game and find out that goalkeepers are to be utilized. At the same time, you don't want to use goalkeepers in practice on a regular basis if they aren't going to be part of the game.

Once you've established that you will, in fact, be using goalkeepers this season, then you must add this to the list of topics to be covered in one of your first practices. Most of your players will be aware of the major difference between goalkeepers and field players—goalkeepers can use their hands. Knowledge and understanding beyond that key point may be limited. Be prepared to educate your players about when and where the goalkeeper can use his hands, basic techniques for catching the ball, and how the goalkeeper gets rid of the ball once he's got it.

Selecting the Goalkeepers

Among the many decisions you will make about your lineup, choosing goalkeepers will likely be one of the most difficult. Although your neighbor may be coaching a team in which every child begs to play in goal, you may have a group exactly the opposite. Don't be surprised if, when you ask for volunteers, your players all take one step backward and begin studying their shoelaces. Whether they are fighting to get in goal or would rather eat broccoli than stand in there, plan to use parts of several practices to determine who is really willing and able to do the job.

The first thing to remember is to not rule anyone out right away (unless there is a medical condition or other safety concern). Being effective in goal takes a unique mentality, which may not show until a player is between the posts. We've seen some of the quietest, meekest children become animals when put in goal. At the same time, some big, tough kids have shown world-class dodgeball skills and searched for mommy when the ball came their way. Start your search with some drills where everyone gets a chance in goal. (Try the shooting drills Everybody keeps, Money ball, and Battle ball from chapter 5.) You can randomly switch the players in, ask for volunteers, or set up a drill where part of the rotation is to jump in goal for a shot or two.

Pay attention to how the players move and the looks on their faces, not just how well they keep the ball out of the net. Although that last part is obviously important, you can get a feel for who is comfortable in goal by watching *how,* rather than just *what,* the players are doing. If their natural instinct is to duck or turn away from the ball, they should slide down the depth chart. You'll have a few kids who get excited about the challenge and enjoy catching the ball or batting it away from the goal. You may also find that a player who isn't strong on the field sees this as an opportunity where she can be successful and contribute to the team.

Overworked and Underpaid

Soccer is a wonderful team sport, but it can be awfully lonely for a goalkeeper. When you win, the goal scorers get most of the glory, and the saves that the keeper made often go uncelebrated. When you lose, missed scoring opportunities are generally forgotten, while the balls missed and dropped by the goalkeeper live on in everyone's mind. It is important that the goalkeepers understand this about the position before taking the field. Help them take pride in the unique and important role they play for the team, and remind all the players that the *team* wins and loses *together.* Encourage the other players to appreciate the goalkeepers and recognize the positive plays they make during the game.

As you begin to get a feel for who the candidates are, try to keep two to four players in your goalkeeping rotation. Do not limit yourself with just one goalkeeper. You never know when someone is going to get sick, get hurt, or miss a game. Having several options also helps ensure that nobody stays in goal for an entire game. Even if they say they just want to be a goalkeeper, kids this age shouldn't be pigeonholed into that select group. All players should be playing multiple positions and learning the skills and concepts needed to play anywhere on the field. Their minds, bodies, and interests will go through a lot of changes over the next 8 to 10 years. The broader their training and understanding of soccer, the better chance that they will still enjoy the game and be excited about playing when they get older.

Designing Practice Opportunities for Goalkeepers

For your goalkeepers to become comfortable and hopefully skillful in goal, they will need a lot of work. The good news is that they should get lots of repetitions whenever you do shooting drills and offensive practices. Help them pick one or two specific points to focus on during those situations so they can work on proper technique. If they are rotating with another keeper, they can watch and learn from one another as well.

When you have an opportunity to work specifically with your keepers, make sure they get plenty of chances to practice simply catching the ball. You can throw or kick the ball to them to give them this practice. Give them a chance to warm up mentally and physically with basic throwing and catching. As they get going, slowly increase the movement or intensity required for them to be successful. When they are ready to be challenged, include balls that require them to move from side to side, reach over their heads, jump, and go down to the ground. Goalkeepers need to be prepared for the fact that the ball won't be coming straight to them during the game. The more practice they get, the better.

Because keepers practice individually or with one or two other players, keep the practice time short, as shown in the sample practice session in figure 7.1. Goalkeeper practices are intense and should last about 15 minutes when working with beginners. If your keepers can't get individual attention during the regular practice, consider having them come a little early or stay after practice occasionally to get some focused training.

Goalkeeping Basics

Being able to dive across the goal, pull a ball out of the upper corner of the goal, or stop penalty kicks are not likely qualifications on your goalkeeper's resume. Remember, you're starting at the very beginning. One of our first goalkeepers was only required to pretend that he wanted to catch the ball. Desire and ability were not synonymous, but he was more willing than anyone else was able. In time, we were able to get both hands moving at the same time, and eventually both eyes moving along with

Figure 7.1 Sample Goalkeeping Practice Plan

Coach: _____ Date: _____

Time: _____

Age group: <u>Any</u>   Theme: <u>15- to 22-minute training</u>
                              <u>session or pregame warm-up</u>

	Duration	Equipment	Activity or drill
Warm-up	3-5 min.	1 ball per goalkeeper	*Bounce and catch* (see page 153) *Stretching*
Goalkeeping activity	2-4 min.	2 balls	*Side to side**: Goalkeeper sits on the ground facing the coach, who has the ball. Toss the ball to the side of the player. The player falls to that side, catching the ball, and rocks back upright, tossing the ball back to you. Continue on the other side. As the player gets warmed up, throw the ball a little harder or a little wider from the keeper.
Goalkeeping activity	3 min.	Several balls, a goal, and a goal box (or cones)	*Two servers* (see page 160)*.
Goalkeeping activity	5-8 min.	5-8 balls	*Shooting repetition***: Gather several soccer balls together near the top of one side of the penalty box. Shoot one ball at a time, allowing the keeper just enough time to make a save and send the ball back. After a series of shots, move to the center of the goal and then to the other side of the box. Progressively increase the intensity of the shots and the amount of movement required to make the save. Consider completing a second round of more challenging shots from farther back.
Cool-down	2 min.		*Stretch* well (players will be sore).

*If working with multiple goalkeepers, switch players after 6-10 tosses.

**If working with multiple goalkeepers, switch players before moving to a new kicking spot.

From L. Blom and T. Blom, 2009, *Survival Guide for Coaching Youth Soccer* (Champaign, IL: Human Kinetics).

both hands. Just as with all the technical and tactical training you plan, patience and persistence will get you through it.

Using basic coaching points for your goalkeepers will go a long way toward helping them improve quickly. The following points may be the only ones you need to make until well into the third or fourth goalkeeping session:

- **Keep the ball out of the goal.** It might seem a little elementary to actually say, "Keep the ball out of the goal," but that is, after all, the main objective. Although you want to help players learn the proper fundamentals, you also don't really care deep down whether it's pretty or ugly as long as the ball stays out of the net. The real foundation for becoming a quality keeper is developing the mentality of reacting and moving quickly in order to prevent a goal. Focusing on the ball, staying light on the feet, and moving into the right position will evolve more naturally if the main priority is simply to keep the ball from going into the goal. Once the keeper has that mind-set, the points you make about her movement and technique will make sense.

- **Remember, you can use your hands.** The best part of being the goalkeeper for your players is that they can use their hands (when it's really, really cold, the best part may be wearing extra layers of clothes). Just like all the players on the field, goalkeepers, by rule, can go anywhere they want. However, they can use their hands only inside the penalty box. On a regulation field, this box extends 18 yards (16 m) from the goal, but smaller fields for the younger age groups are often lined differently. Again, you should check the specific guidelines for your league so you can help your players understand where goalkeepers are allowed to use their hands. When goalkeepers are outside that area, they are regulated by the same rules as the other field players.

  Rarely will your goalkeepers find themselves outside the penalty area. However, there are still restrictions on when they can use their hands within that boundary. Goalkeepers are not allowed to pick up balls that are intentionally passed to them by a teammate or balls that are trapped to the ground by a teammate. In other words, if a defender gains control of the ball, he can't kick it to the goalkeeper or leave it for the goalkeeper to pick up. If a ball is *intentionally* played from a teammate to the goalkeeper, including on a throw-in, the goalkeeper must play the ball as a field player (no hands). The result of breaking this rule is an indirect free kick for the other team.

  Emphasis on the word *intentionally* is not meant to encourage you to be sneaky and try to get around the rule. It is to emphasize that players often misplay the ball, and the goalkeeper is allowed to use her hands if that happens. If a defender tries to clear a ball, for example, and he shanks it out in front of his own goal, the goalkeeper can catch it or pick it up. This often happens when a player is running toward a ball rolling toward him or a ball that is bouncing. As long as the player doesn't deliberately kick it to the goalkeeper, the ball can be played with the hands. Keep in mind that your perception of *intentional* and the referee's interpretation may differ. During such a moment, remember that you are the coach, you are the adult, and you are modeling proper behavior for your players. Besides, complaining about the call is likely to accomplish nothing. If you complain to the officials and they change the call, notify local media outlets at once!

Once you have covered the "keep the ball out of the goal" and "use your hands" part of goalkeeping, you can move on to the next level of tips. Sam Snow, U.S. Youth Soccer director of coaching, encourages coaches to focus on these points*:

- **Go for everything.** In time, your goalkeepers will begin to find their range, or comfort zone, for how far out they can go for the ball and how quickly they can move off their line to beat an opponent to the ball. Encourage them to take chances, and help them process good decision making. Provide opportunities during practice for them to work on this so they aren't just guessing during the game.

- **Communicate loudly.** When the goalkeeper comes out to make a save, pick up the ball, or catch a cross, she should call for the ball. Shouting her own name or screaming, "Keeper!" lets members of her team know to get out of the way and lets the opponent know that the goalkeeper is coming for the ball. A goalkeeper who communicates with confidence will face fewer challenges from the opposition.

- **Give 100 percent effort.** When the choice is made to come out for a ball, the goalkeeper must fully commit to that decision. Any hesitation after that point makes him more vulnerable to giving up a goal or maybe even getting hurt. The same is true for simply reaching to catch a ball or diving on the ground. It is important that the goalkeeper stay focused and put full effort into these movements so he is ready for any twists, turns, falls, or other impacts.

- **After a save, get up quickly.** Once the save is made or attempted, the goalkeeper should get up quickly and find the ball, if she doesn't have it in her hands. She should be looking as she gets up and preparing to make another save. If she does have the ball in her hands, tell her to distribute it before celebrating the save. In most leagues, the goalkeeper has 6 seconds to release the ball after making a save or gaining possession. We discuss distribution tips later in the chapter.

- **No moping.** Tell your players to move on with the game after a goal is scored. Work to instill in the goalkeepers the idea that they need to be focused on the present and quickly move on from any mistakes or bad breaks.

*Adapted, by permission, from S. Snow, n.d., *Cardinal rules of goalkeeping*. [Online]. Available: http://www.usyouthsoccer.org/doc_lib/Cardinal_Rules_of_Goalkeeping.pdf [January 5, 2009].

Catching and Hand Position

Ideally, the goalkeeper should move his hands as if he is wearing handcuffs. As the right hand moves, the left hand goes with it, and vice versa. The keeper should also catch the ball with both hands. There should be one sound when the hands meet the ball rather than the pitter-patter of one hand hitting just before the other. The objective should be to catch the ball, not to bounce it, bat it down, or push it away. There will be times when a save can be made only by hitting the ball away, but most of the time, the keeper should catch a ball that he can reach with both hands.

If the ball is above the waist, the goalkeeper should catch the ball with his hands up, with fingers toward the sky and thumbs side by side (see figure 7.2*a*). If the ball is at the waist or lower, including a ball on the ground, the keeper should catch the ball with his hands down, with fingers pointed down and pinkie fingers next to one another (see figure 7.2*b*). As he catches the ball, he should cushion it and pull it in to his body, which helps control and protect the ball (figure 7.2*c*).

Figure 7.2   The proper technique for goalkeepers includes (*a*) fingers pointed up for balls above the waist, (*b*) fingers pointed down for balls below the waist, and (*c*) cushioning and pulling the ball in to the body.

When the ball is rolling on the ground, the goalkeeper should bend the knees while leaning forward to pick it up (see figure 7.3). If the ball is rolling quickly or the ground is bumpy or wet, it is easy to mishandle the ball. So, teach your goalkeeper to bend one knee so that it is close to the ground as if she is getting ready to kneel. To get one knee close to the ground, the other knee will be bent as well. This allows the goalkeeper to get close to the ground and get her body behind the ball, while still preventing it from rolling underneath her legs. Encourage the keeper when possible to avoid actually placing a knee all the way down on the ground. She needs to still be able to shift her weight, move side to side, and quickly follow any dropped balls, and this is more easily accomplished if the weight and balance of the body are still on her feet rather than a knee.

Figure 7.3　Proper technique for a goalkeeper to stop a rolling ball.

Whether a shot comes on the ground or in the air, it is crucial that the keeper have her entire body behind the ball. Whenever the opponent has the ball within shooting range, the goalkeeper should have her hands up, palms out, a little below chest level. When her hands are in this position, she is already halfway to a save. A goalkeeper who stands with her hands hanging by her sides has to pick them up and get them together before she can catch a ball.

Body Positioning and Stance

It doesn't matter how great your goalkeeper's hands are if he doesn't get into the right position to get them on the ball. The goalkeeper should maintain a ready position so he is prepared to react to a shot at all times. Because the field is often short in small-sided soccer, shots can accidentally or intentionally be taken from most anywhere on the field. You want your keeper to be ready to go; surprises are not a good thing for goalkeepers.

In the ready position, the keeper should be forward on his feet, which are about shoulder-width apart, maybe a little wider, with his knees bent. Help each goalkeeper find a comfortable stance; this may vary slightly depending on the size and shape of the player. His hands should be up in front of the chest with arms slightly bent, fingers pointing up, and palms facing out toward the field. Remind him to keep his eyes on the ball. He should be following the ball as it moves across the field so he is ready for a shot (this idea also keeps him from picking the weeds that are inside the goal or watching kids on other fields).

A big part of being successful in goal is moving to make the goal harder for the opponent to hit. When the ball is on the other end of the field, the keeper should move out toward the top of the box. If the opposing team clears a ball down the field, the keeper may be able to pick up the ball or run out and send it up to a teammate before an opponent can get to it. As the other team moves down the field with the ball, the goalkeeper can move back closer to the goal. If the other team is in shooting range, the keeper should be in ready position.

Any movement forward and backward should be done facing out onto the field. The goalkeeper should never turn his back on the ball. As the opposing team moves across the field, the goalkeeper should shuffle across the goal without crossing his feet, always keeping his hands up, prepared to make a save. The idea is to be positioned at an angle to take up as much of the goal as possible (see figure 7.4). He should be close enough to the near post (the side of the goal nearest to the ball) to attempt a save on that side. At the same time, the keeper should be angled so that he can get to a ball played across the goal to the far post. Coach your goalkeepers to have their hands ready for a shot and their feet ready to move across the goal in case there is a pass or cross. Staying light on his feet will help him change directions quickly and jump or dive, if necessary.

Figure 7.4 The goalkeeper should be positioned at an angle to take up as much space as possible and make the goal smaller for the shooter.

Diving

Lie down on the floor on your belly. Seriously, lie down. Raise your arms as far as you can. You probably can't reach very far (and you probably aren't very comfortable). Now, put your arms back down and get up as fast as you can. You used both hands and both feet and probably both knees. Now lie down on your side. Notice that the arm and leg on top are free to move, swing, and reach well into the air. If you were in goal, your range would be much better on your side than on your belly. In this position, you are also still facing forward (out onto the field). Now, stand up as fast as you can. One arm and one leg should have done the trick. If not, remember that your players are younger and may be more agile than you, and one leg and arm will likely work for them. This leaves the other leg and arm still available to reach and deflect a shot.

Here's what you've just demonstrated: If keepers do have to go to the ground, they should go down on the side rather than the abdomen. The natural instinct for many young players is the Superman dive across the goal. There are several problems with this approach: (1) They are essentially doing a belly flop onto the ground, increasing the risk for injury (or at least the risk of knocking the wind or breakfast out of themselves); (2) if they are lying on their bellies, they probably can't get both hands on the ball; and (3) they can't reach for a ball that bounces or gets deflected above or behind them.

Instead, keepers should collapse to the ground on their sides rather than fall on their bellies. They should fall with arms together and extended (see figure 7.5). They should attack the ball with their hands and let the body fall without using their hands or elbows to catch themselves. As previously noted, they should catch the ball with both hands (still in

Figure 7.5 When diving for a ball, the goalkeeper should extend his arms, catch the ball with both hands, and land on his side.

handcuffs) and pull the ball to the chest after catching it. Talk to your goalkeepers about the correct form for diving, and discuss the benefits of doing it properly. If it makes sense to them, they are more likely to practice doing it right and to be prepared as they grow as keepers.

Distribution

Once your team gains possession of the ball, you want to keep it. That doesn't change when the goalkeeper has the ball. Ideally, she'll get the ball to a teammate, who can then begin the process of attacking the other team. The most common way for a goalkeeper to distribute the ball to her teammates is by punting it down the field. When punting the ball, the goalkeeper drops it out of her hands and then kicks it before it hits the ground. This typically results in the farthest possible distance, but it is sometimes difficult to be accurate. With practice, goalkeepers should be able to kick the ball in the general vicinity of their teammates. Initially, the aim should be down the field, closer to the sidelines than the middle of the field.

If punting isn't really working out for your keeper, she is allowed to put the ball on the ground and then kick it down the field. The biggest benefit here is that she is essentially passing it like a field player, so she should be more accurate than when punting. However, once she puts the ball on the ground, she can't pick it back up. She is now essentially a field player, and the other team could pressure her and try to win the ball.

Another option for distributing the ball is for the goalkeeper to throw it in the air or roll the ball on the ground. Throwing the ball is helpful when the goalkeeper needs to send the ball over opponents to a teammate who is fairly close by. Unfortunately a thrown ball will bounce when it hits the ground, making it harder for the field player to control. Rolling the ball is helpful when a teammate is open and fairly close to the goalkeeper. If the keeper rolls the ball, the teammate on the other end can receive it more easily and quickly head up the field. With older players, throwing the ball can be a pretty good weapon because of their ability to be very accurate. Young players often struggle here because the ball is too big for them. In general, if they can't throw the ball with one hand, they aren't ready to throw it out to their teammates. But they might still be able to roll it.

Ideally, when a goalkeeper kicks, throws, or rolls the ball out to a teammate, the objective is the same as when making a quality pass. The player receiving the ball should get it on or close to the ground at a pace that is firm but easy to control. As a coach, you have to decide if you will encourage possession by having the goalkeeper send the ball to a teammate who is fairly close, or if it is better just to have the keeper punt the ball down the field and then let teammates fight to win it there. This will depend on both the ability of the goalkeeper and the comfort level of the other players on the field.

Breakaways

Among the most terrifying experiences for most young goalkeepers is the dreaded breakaway. In the younger age groups, this shouldn't happen very often because the field isn't long enough, and the players don't play the ball fast enough to create one-on-one opportunities. As they get older, goalkeepers will be trained more specifically on the proper timing for coming out to the ball and cutting down the space and angles of the attacking player. For your goalkeepers, limit your coaching for breakaway situations to the following directives:

- Stay light on your feet, ready to react to the play.
- Keep your hands up so they are already in position to make a save.
- Make your body big by raising your elbows slightly from the side and keeping a stance slightly wider than shoulder width.
- Watch for opportunities to win the ball before the shot, such as when the dribbling player touches the ball a little too far in front.

A common mistake that young goalkeepers make is focusing on the opponent rather than the ball. Who can blame kids for worrying about getting run over or getting their teeth knocked out? However, if they focus on watching the ball and attacking the ball, they are ultimately less likely to be in harm's way when they challenge the opposition. When their focus is on the ball, they will react quickly and often get to the ball before the opponent. They won't believe this at first, but quite often a goalkeeper who confidently attacks a loose ball will intimidate the other players from making a play.

Drill 1 Bounce and Catch

Skill warm-up, pregame warm-up

EQUIPMENT
1 ball for every goalkeeper

PLAYING AREA
A 5- × 5-yard (5 × 5 m) area, but grid lines are not needed

PURPOSE
Teaching ball-handling skills

PROCEDURE
Each goalkeeper has a ball in hand. Using both hands, players bounce the ball off the ground and catch it with the correct form. Players repeatedly bounce the ball 15 to 25 times while skipping around a small area.

MODIFICATIONS
Players can bounce the ball between their legs, turn, and catch the ball with the correct form. Players can pound the ball into the ground with their fists and then catch it.

Drill 2 Ball Work

Skill warm-up, pregame warm-up

EQUIPMENT
1 ball for every goalkeeper

PLAYING AREA
No specific playing area

PURPOSE
Teaching ball-handling skills

PROCEDURE
Each goalkeeper has a ball in hand. Players complete the following tasks, repeating them in sets of 10:

- Roll the ball on the ground in a figure-eight motion around the legs (see photos).
- Swing the ball in the air in a figure-eight motion around the legs.
- Hold the ball with both hands behind the head, drop it, and catch it behind the back with both hands.

Drill 3 Sit, Throw, Jump, Catch

Skill warm-up, pregame warm-up

EQUIPMENT
1 ball for every goalkeeper

PLAYING AREA
Enough space for the players to jump up without running into each other

PURPOSE
Teaching ball handling and improving jumping, agility, and reaction time

PROCEDURE
Players sit on the ground while holding a ball. They toss the ball into the air about 5 to 8 feet (1.5 to 2.5 m) and then jump up and catch it with proper form.

COACHING POINTS
Remind your players to keep their eyes on the ball, use both hands with thumbs side by side when catching the ball, get up off the ground quickly, call, "Keeper!" when they commit to going after the ball, and catch the ball at the highest point possible.

MODIFICATIONS
Players can start on their backs or on the ground with legs crossed or straight out in front.

Drill 4 Crunch and Catch

Skill warm-up, pregame warm-up

EQUIPMENT
1 ball for every 2 goalkeepers

PLAYING AREA
5- × 10-yard (5 × 9 m) rectangle

PURPOSE
Teaching ball handling and throwing

PROCEDURE
Pair players, and have them sit facing each other about 2 to 3 yards (2 to 3 m) apart. If the number of goalkeepers isn't even, you can act as a partner. Players sit in a crunchlike position (legs out in front, knees bent, feet flat on ground). Goalkeeper 1 throws the ball with an overhand two-hand throw to goalkeeper 2, who catches the ball with the proper form, lies back on the ground, and comes back up to a sitting position (like a sit-up). Goalkeeper 2 then throws the ball back using the same form, and goalkeeper 1 completes the sit-up movement. Repeat 10 to 15 times. The next progression is for goalkeeper 1 to stand and toss the ball to each side (right, then left) of goalkeeper 2 so the sit-up is done to the side rather than straight up. The players repeat 10 to 15 times and switch roles.

COACHING POINTS

Players should use proper technique when catching the ball. Remind them to fall to the side when diving (rather than on their bellies) and to rock back up quickly.

MODIFICATIONS

Goalkeeper 1 stands and tosses the ball to each side (right, then left) of goalkeeper 2, who is squatting 2 to 3 yards (2 to 3 m) away. Goalkeeper 2 is now diving to the side from a slightly higher point. After 4 to 6 repetitions on each side, the players switch roles.

Drill 5 Partner Pride

Skill warm-up, pregame warm-up

EQUIPMENT
1 ball for every 2 goalkeepers

PLAYING AREA
10- × 10-yard (9 × 9 m) area

PURPOSE
Teaching proper ball handling, footwork, and diving technique

PROCEDURE
Players kneel on the ground facing each other about 3 to 5 yards (3 to 5 m) away. Players roll and toss the ball back and forth, working on proper technique using the following progression of tasks. After working through each of the four stages while kneeling, the players should stand and repeat the progression.

- Goalkeeper 1 rolls the ball straight toward goalkeeper 2, who scoops up the ball using the correct form. Goalkeeper 2 rolls the ball back straight toward goalkeeper 1, who also scoops up the ball. Players repeat 10 times.

- Goalkeeper 1 rolls the ball to the side of goalkeeper 2, who correctly falls to the side and catches the ball with both hands. Goalkeeper 2 rolls the ball back to the side of goalkeeper 1, who falls to the side to catch the ball. Players alternate rolling the ball to the right and left side of their partners. Players repeat 5 times on each side.

- Players throw the ball with both hands straight to their partners, who use the correct form to catch the ball: thumbs together for balls above the waist and pinkies together for balls falling below the waist. Players repeat 10 times.

- Players throw the ball with both hands to each side of their partners, who catch the ball, falling to the ground with correct diving form (see photo). Players repeat 5 times on each side.

Drill 6 Two Servers

Skill warm-up, pregame warm-up

EQUIPMENT
Several balls; a goal; a goal box (or 6 cones)

PLAYING AREA
Use the goal box, or if you do not have an actual goal to use, use four cones to set up a rectangle similar in size to the goal box that is used in your league for this age group. Use two cones to mark a goal.

PURPOSE
Teaching ball handling and footwork while in motion

PROCEDURE
This drill includes two servers and at least one goalkeeper. The servers stand 5 to 10 yards (5 to 9 m) in front of the goal, lined up with opposite goalposts. The goalkeeper shuffles back and forth across the goal to receive a ball from the server. Servers can roll, throw, bounce, or volley the ball toward the goalkeeper. Servers should mix up the types of services, from on the ground to high in the air. Players repeat this 10 to 15 times. After a sufficient break, repeat the drill. If you have two goalkeepers, have them shuffle to opposite goalposts, passing each other in the middle of the goal between serves. The servers will serve at the same time to each goalkeeper.

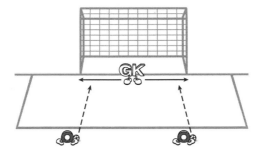

MODIFICATIONS
Ask goalkeepers to say, "Keeper!" when they start moving toward the ball. Have players do a push-up, jumping jack, or somersault before shuffling across the goal. Place a cone at an angle that the goalkeepers have to shuffle around before receiving the next ball.

Drill 7 Attack the Ball

Skill warm-up, skill training

EQUIPMENT
2 balls for every group of 3 players; enough cones to mark the area

PLAYING AREA
A grid about 10 × 15 yards (9 × 14 m)

PURPOSE
Teaching proper technique for handling, smothering, and diving in game-like situations; teaching players to communicate and be aggressive

PROCEDURE
All three players are in the grid. Two players dribble around the grid. The third player is designated as the goalkeeper. The goalkeeper, on your command, stretches out to dive on one of the balls, taking it from the feet of one of the dribbling players. Remind dribblers that they cannot touch the ball once it is in the goalkeeper's possession. Players repeat 10 times and switch roles.

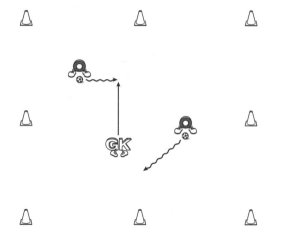

COACHING POINTS
Remind the goalkeepers to protect the ball with their bodies so it does not slip out from underneath them.

Drill 8 Long Kicks and Throws

Skill training

EQUIPMENT
1 ball for every 2 goalkeepers; 10 cones

PLAYING AREA
20- x 30-yard (18 x 27 m) rectangle; use the cones to mark off the area and to create a goal at each end

PURPOSE
Teaching technique for goal kicks, punts, and throws

PROCEDURE
Goalkeepers are paired. They should stand at the ends of the rectangle. One goalkeeper starts with the ball and kicks a goal kick to the other goalkeeper, who uses correct form to catch the ball or pick it up off the ground. Then, that player takes a goal kick back to the first goalkeeper. Goalkeepers can punt the ball (make grid bigger) or throw the ball to work on other forms of distributing the ball.

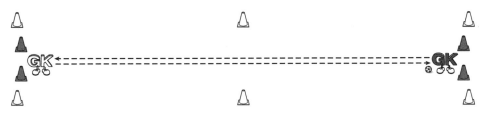

MODIFICATIONS
Vary the distance of the rectangle. Make the rectangle narrow, and award points for good kicks or throws that stay inbounds.

Drill 9 1v1

Skill training

EQUIPMENT
1 ball at a time (have several extra balls)

PLAYING AREA
10- × 10-yard (9 × 9 m) grid for every pair of players; goals 4 yards (4 m) wide placed on opposite sides or ends

PURPOSE
Teaching ball handling and footwork in gamelike situations

PROCEDURE
Players should work in pairs. Each player defends a goal. One player starts with the ball and rolls it with force toward the other player's goal, with the intention to score. Players score points for saving a goal with the correct form. Play to 10 points.

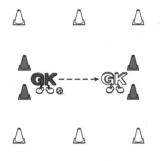

MODIFICATIONS
Players can throw or bounce the ball toward the other goal.

Drill 10 Circle Catches

Team training

EQUIPMENT
1 ball for every field player

PLAYING AREA
An area about 15 × 15 yards (14 × 14 m) to 20 × 20 yards (18 × 18 m)

PURPOSE
Teaching proper technique for footwork, ball handling, and distribution

PROCEDURE
Organize one goalkeeper and five to seven field players in groups. Have the field players stand in a circle, with the goalkeeper in the middle about 10 yards (9 m) from all players. Each field player needs a ball. When you yell out the name of a field player, the player responds by saying, "Ball." The goalkeeper turns toward that player, and the player chips or passes the ball toward her. Emphasize to players that they are not trying to score on the goalkeeper; rather, they are just passing the ball toward her. (If the players are having trouble passing with accuracy, have them throw or bounce the ball rather than kick it). The goalkeeper handles the ball with correct form and distributes it back to the player. Call another player's name to repeat the drill. Repeat these steps 10 to 15 times. Rotate players into the middle to be the goalkeeper.

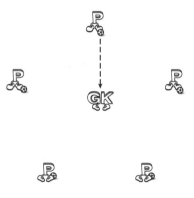

COACHING POINTS
Instruct the goalkeeper to quickly turn toward the player who has been identified as the kicker. After receiving the ball, the keeper rolls the ball with accuracy toward the player's feet.

MODIFICATIONS
Players can dribble around, rather than stand, in the grid while the goalkeeper jogs around and finds the identified player. Upon your command the player kicks the ball toward the goalkeeper who uses correct form to catch the ball and then rolls it back to the player.

The Coach's Clipboard

✔ When selecting goalkeepers, start with drills that give everyone an opportunity to play in goal. Look for players who seem to feel comfortable in goal.

✔ Remember that goalkeeper-specific practices are intense, so keep them short (about 15 minutes).

✔ When you start the initial training of your goalkeepers, focus on having them use their hands to keep the ball out of the goal.

✔ Goalkeepers can use their hands inside the penalty box, but they may not pick up balls that have been intentionally passed back to them by a teammate.

✔ Encourage your goalkeepers to communicate loudly when going after a ball.

✔ Goalkeepers should catch the ball with both hands together as if wearing handcuffs. For balls caught below the waist, the pinkie fingers should be together; for balls caught above the waist, the thumbs should be together.

✔ Instruct your goalkeepers to cushion the ball as they catch it and then to bring it in to the chest.

✔ When diving for balls, goalkeepers should fall to their side with their arms extended together.

Teaching Restart and Heading Skills With 10 Simple Drills

Soccer is a game of flow. There are no time-outs and very few breaks in the action. The main reasons for stoppage of play in soccer are when the ball goes out of bounds or when a foul is committed. At the youngest age groups, the ball goes out of bounds far more often than fouls are called. Most referees have the good sense to know that these kids are going to be running into each other and falling down all the time. Unless there appears to be an intentional foul or a complete disregard for safety, there probably won't be too many fouls whistled. The one exception to this may be hand balls. There will be *lots* of these. During the season you will encounter some referees who exercise selective vision and ignore any hand ball that doesn't include actually catching the ball, and you will see referees who believe that stopping play every 45 seconds is the best way to reinforce the rules and teach the kids to not use their hands.

With each stoppage of play, there is an accompanying restart. When a ball goes out of bounds, the team that did not touch it last gets to restart the play. If the ball goes out over the sideline, play is restarted with a throw-in. If the ball goes out over the end line, play is restarted with either a goal kick or corner kick. If the ball goes out off of the offensive team, like on a missed shot, the defensive team takes a goal kick. If a defensive player, including the goalkeeper, is the last to touch the ball, then play is restarted with a corner kick. At the higher levels of soccer, corner kicks present fantastic scoring opportunities. For the younger age groups, seek out a player who can kick the ball from the corner to the front of the goal.

Free kicks are restarts that take place after a foul or violation of the rules. If your team is not within realistic shooting range, emphasize keeping possession of the ball. On the other hand, if the free kick takes place in front of the opponent's goal, then you should look to shoot. The most important factor in taking an effective free kick or in defending a free kick is paying attention and getting into position quickly.

In addition to these types of restarts, the game, the second half, and each quarter in some leagues begin with a kickoff. (Be sure to check the rules for your league to find out if quarters are started with a kickoff or if they start where the play ended at the termination of the previous quarter.) Kickoffs take place in the middle of the field, with each team set up on its own side. Once the ball is in play, the clock starts and doesn't stop again until the end of the quarter or half (unless there is an injury). After a goal is scored, the team that gives up the goal restarts play with a kickoff.

This chapter also includes information about headers. Although headers are not used to restart the ball, they are a unique skill that requires a different practice design than the skills discussed in the other chapters of this book.

You will not need to spend an entire practice on any of these skills, so you can incorporate the 10 drills in this chapter into a warm-up or complete a few at the end of practice. For example, during a practice where the focus is on passing, you could include a drill or two in which players take free kicks or corner kicks. Set up the drill so the player restarting the play has a specific target player or place on the field to which she is trying to get the ball. To practice throw-ins, require that players who are serving the ball to a teammate during a drill use proper throw-in technique rather than simply tossing the ball randomly. During a skill warm-up or skill practice, include a rotation in which the players head the ball to a teammate.

KISS

You've probably heard the phrase and acronym "keep it simple, stupid" (KISS). If you had a teacher like the sweet lady who taught my third-grade math class, you were taught to keep it simple, sweetheart. If you were on my ninth-grade football team, then the last *S* may be replaced by any number of colorful words. The point either way is to fight the urge to get too creative with your restarts. Keep it simple, Supercoach. The more passes that must be made during a particular restart, the more chances there are for one to go astray. The more players involved in a play, the more opportunities there are for someone to forget their role. Your strategy should be based on one of these three desirable outcomes:

- Create a scoring opportunity.
- Maintain possession of the ball.
- Get the ball directly down the field.

The time of the game when the restart occurs, the score of the game, the level of the opposition, and the ability of your own players may all be factors in selecting which of these three outcomes is the most important at a given time.

Kickoffs

At the start of each half (or quarters for some leagues) and after a goal is scored, a kickoff is used to start play. For this kick, the ball is placed on the center spot inside the center circle at midfield. A coin toss is typically used to determine who has the kickoff to start the game; the other team will have the kickoff to start the next period. When a goal is scored, the team who got scored on takes the kickoff.

Here are the rules of the kickoff:

- All players must be on their half of the field before the ball is kicked, including the forwards on each team.
- The defensive team (the team not taking the kickoff) must be outside the center circle.
- The stationary ball must be kicked forward before it is officially in play.
- The player who kicked the ball cannot touch it again until someone else touches it. In other words, the player cannot dribble the ball down the field.

Because of these rules, typically two players on the offensive team will stand near the ball to take the kickoff (see figure 8.1). One player will gently roll or tap the ball slightly forward, and then the other player takes control of the ball. The ball can then be passed or dribbled. Although there are many complex plays designed for kickoffs, we recommend sending the ball down the field toward the goal, or at least down the sideline. Teams often elect to pass the ball back into their defensive end but then end up losing possession. In this instance, the opponent now has the ball in front of the goal instead of the kickoff team having the ball down in front of their attacking goal. This is a waste of a good offensive opportunity. With a kickoff, the ball is already halfway down the field, so use that to your advantage. Keep possession of it, and move it forward toward the attacking goal. The best way to practice kickoffs is to incorporate them into practice scrimmages.

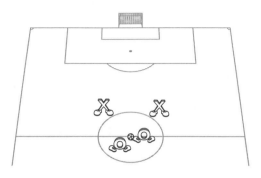
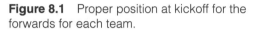

Figure 8.1   Proper position at kickoff for the forwards for each team.

Goal Kicks

When the attacking team plays the ball over the opponent's end line (the goal line), a goal kick is awarded to the defending team. For a goal kick, the ball must be placed inside the goal box if the age group is playing with goalkeepers. If you are not playing with goalkeepers, the ball is typically placed on the field 2 to 3 yards (2 to 3 m) from the end line. Any player on the field can take a goal kick, but typically the goalkeeper or defenders are given this duty so the rest of the players are available out on the field to help maintain your team's shape. Plus, when everyone knows this is the keeper's job, the other players won't fight for the opportunity. Teach your goalkeepers how to take these kicks, even if at first they are not your best kickers. If you are unsure of their accuracy, have a defender stand in the goal until the goalkeepers can return to their position.

The ball must be kicked out of the penalty box before the ball is touched again. If the ball doesn't make it out of the penalty box, the kick must be retaken. Using the technique for a driven pass (see chapter 4), the kicker should direct the ball high and wide to avoid the attacking opponents. A ball played down the middle of the field is likely to be intercepted and leaves the team vulnerable to a quick attack. If the ball is not kicked high enough, it will hit the defenders or attackers instead of traveling down the field. The outside midfielders and strikers should move into a helpful position so the kicker has a target area and teammates to help receive the ball.

Corner Kicks

When the ball goes out of bounds over the end line off of a defensive player, the game is restarted with a corner kick. An offensive player plays the ball in from the corner of the field. As with all the other restarts, once the player taking the corner kick strikes the ball, he can't hit it again until another player has made contact with the ball. Other offensive players should be positioned inside the penalty box, ready to move to the ball when it is sent into play. Defensive players should be matched up with an opponent to try to win the ball and clear it out of the area. This often resembles the first 15 seconds after a pinata bursts open at a birthday party. Because of the traffic and the number of players in a small area, offensive players should be encouraged to shoot as soon as they have an opening. Likewise, defensive players should move to the ball and clear it out immediately.

Offensively, your team really has two good options to create a solid goal-scoring opportunity. The player taking the corner kick can cross it out in front of the goal (see Basic corner on page 187) or pass the ball to a teammate who is close by (see Short corner on page 188). The benefit of a cross is that the ball is in front of the opponent's goal (this is typically a good place to be if you are on offense). The downside of a crossed ball is that you risk losing possession, and you may not have any players willing or able to get in front of the ball to redirect it into the goal. On the other hand, if your player passes the ball in to a teammate, your team maintains possession but needs to work harder to get the ball into scoring range. Dedicate some practice time early in the season to allow players to practice crossing the ball and shooting the ball on goal from these crosses. When working on crosses and corner kicks from an offensive standpoint, focus on the following key ideas:

- The crosser should try to play the ball into the space where her teammates are running.
- The crosser should try to play the ball just out of the goalkeeper's range.
- Players should start out away from the goal and run in rather than just camp out right in front of the goal.
- Players should try to time their runs so they are still moving as the ball comes into their area.

- Players trying to receive the ball should position themselves with the cross so the path of the ball intersects the path of their run.

- If a player is not in position to receive a cross, he should frame the goal by moving just outside the post and preparing to redirect any shots that go just wide. In other words, if a player realizes he won't be getting the ball, he can move into a position next to the goalpost, just to the outside. He should position himself so he can see the ball, so if a teammate shoots it, he can try to direct the ball into the goal or at least follow the shot.

- Position players in different spaces within the area in front of the goal, and keep a defender or two back toward midfield to challenge for a ball that gets cleared out of the box.

The strategy for defending the corner kick is simple: Get to the ball first, and get it away from the goal. Each defensive player should mark a player on the opposing team. If you have extra players, send one up toward midfield to serve as an outlet or to fight for any ball that gets cleared out of the box. Other extra players could cover one of the posts of the goal. This player stands on the goal line on the inside of a post and kicks the ball if it comes near. A player positioned on the post can make the goal smaller by covering the hard-to-reach places for the goalkeeper. It is worthwhile to remind these players that they can't use their hands even though they are standing right in front of the goal.

Communication is a crucial component of corner kicks. The player taking the corner should signal her teammates that she is about to strike the ball. Anyone trying to make a play on the cross should call for the ball so her teammates know to stay out of her way and prepare to back her up. Defensively, players should call for the ball so they don't all commit and leave other players open. If the goalkeeper can get to the ball, she should call for it and then move aggressively to the ball.

A typical offensive formation for corner kicks is to line up one player on the ball, with several other players lined up at or near the top of the penalty box. When the player taking the kick approaches the ball, the players at the top of the box each make different runs (one to the near post, one to the far post, and one to the middle of the goal). There should also be a player who stays at the top of the box. This player should react to the play and try to keep the ball in front of the goal.

Free Kicks

When a foul occurs or when there is some other type of rules violation, the game is restarted with a free kick. A free kick is a free opportunity to play the ball. During a free kick, the defending team must be a minimum of 10 yards (9 m) away from the ball. (Check your league's rules because the distance may be different for younger age groups playing on smaller fields.) The extra space between the ball and the defenders allows the kicker an opening for a shot or time to make an accurate pass to a teammate. Take advantage of this opportunity by coaching your kids to pay attention to the opponent, watch for good shooting opportunities, and communicate with their teammates as the play develops.

For the purpose of creating a strategy for your free kicks, there are essentially two areas on the field where a free kick may be awarded: within shooting range of your opponent's goal or outside of shooting range of your opponent's goal. If your team is near the opponent's goal when a foul is called, encourage your players to try to take a shot. A common formation is to have two players stand at the ball and several other offensive players in the box, preparing to follow the shot (see Basic free kicks on page 190). One of the players shoots, the others follow the ball. If you are not realistically in range to take a good shot, work to keep possession of the ball so you can get into range to take a good shot.

There are two different kinds of free kicks: direct and indirect. A direct kick can be shot directly into the goal. Pushing, tripping, and other contact fouls result in direct kicks. A hand ball also warrants a direct free kick. Other, lesser infractions result in indirect free kicks. These may include obstruction (getting in the way of a player but not trying to play the ball), dangerous play (kicking at a ball up in the air near another player's face or trying to play the ball while lying on the ground), or other nonviolent fouls. The referee will typically tell the players on the field whether the free kick is direct or indirect. The proper referee signal that distinguishes an indirect kick from a direct kick is a raised arm. The official will raise one arm straight up and lower it when a second player has touched the ball. With an indirect kick, the ball must be touched by two players before going into the net (see figure 8.2). If you have two players on the ball, one can make a short pass to set the other up for a shot. Again, the other players should be prepared to follow the shot.

During practice, watch for players who are naturally scrappy in and around the goal. There are usually one or two players who have a knack for finding the ball and scoring garbage goals. These are the

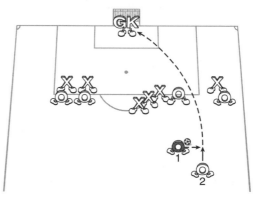

Figure 8.2 For an indirect free kick, the ball must be touched by two players before it goes into the goal. One of the two players standing at the ball can pass to the other player who can then take the shot.

players you want following the free kicks. Your best or most accurate shooters should be positioned on the ball. If you have the luxury of a good left-footed shooter, it is a bonus to have one right-footed player and one left-footed player line up prepared to shoot. That scenario is difficult for a goalkeeper to read and defend. Keep the actual play very simple, but practice it several times so everyone is comfortable with where to go and what to do. You may have certain players involved when you are very close to the goal, and others for balls that are farther away from the goal.

If a foul occurs inside the penalty box, the team is awarded a penalty kick (PK). Be aware that penalty kicks are typically awarded only in age groups using goalkeepers. In this case, the defense is not allowed to set up in front of the ball. In fact, the only players allowed inside the box are the goalkeeper and one shooter from the offensive team. All other players must be outside the penalty area. On a regulation soccer field, the ball is placed 12 yards (11 m) out from the goal (closer on smaller fields). This spot is typically marked with a painted dot or small stripe.

The goalkeeper starts in goal, standing on the goal line. He can bounce up and down or shift side to side, but he is not supposed to move off the line until the shot is taken. The referee blows his whistle to start the play, and the shooter gets one free shot on goal. As soon as the shot is taken, the other players on the field are allowed to follow the shot. Penalty kicks are a nerve-racking part of the game, because all the attention is on the goalkeeper and the lone shooter. Practice this scenario throughout the season so your players can get used to the uniqueness of the situation. Your more experienced and confident players will typically be your best penalty kick takers.

When defending a free kick, the most important thing is to pay attention and be prepared to react quickly to the situation. If the other team is in position to take a shot, consider putting a player or two in front of the ball. Remember, these players have to be 10 yards (9 m) back or whatever distance is mandated for the age group in your league. Defensive players line up in front of the ball to form what is often referred to as a *wall*. The purpose of a wall is to cut off part of the goal so the goalkeeper has less area to cover. The wall typically lines up in front of the ball, but off centered toward the nearer post. The goalkeeper can then shift toward the far post and take a better angle for any potential shots. Setting up a wall could be introduced at the U8 age group with two or three players standing together. Otherwise, one player in front of the ball to stop any low shots and react to any short passes is sufficient.

Players who are not lined up in front of the ball should each mark a player from the opposing team. They should also follow any shots that are taken and try to clear the ball out of the penalty area as quickly as possible. Be sure to practice defensive free kicks so the players need only limited instruction during the game. If the coach is directing traffic during the game, the players will be focused on the sideline, not the actual play on the field. Use the following key points when teaching your players to defend a free kick:

- Players should get into position behind the ball quickly and keep their eyes on the ball.
- Each player should mark a player from the other team and try to stay between that player and the goal.
- Players should clear the ball far and wide, up the sideline if possible.
- Players must communicate when going to the ball. If multiple players are swinging for the ball at the same time, there is a good chance that nobody will actually clear it out.
- Every player should listen to her teammates, especially to the goalkeeper.

Throw-Ins

When the ball goes out of bounds on the side of the field (at the touch line, or sideline), it is put back in play with an over-the-head throw. This is the only time the field players are allowed to use their hands. The team who did not knock the ball out of bounds is awarded a throw-in. Players who are inexperienced passers often accidentally kick the ball out of bounds, and players who are new at receiving the ball will mishandle it, knocking it out of bounds. So, if your team or your opponent is still perfecting these skills, there will likely be many throw-ins during a game. It is not out of the question to be awarded as many as 20 throw-ins a game. Depending on the length of the game, that may be as much as one almost every minute. It may even seem as if your players are throwing the ball in more than they are using their feet.

Your players will think that throw-ins are special because they get to break the no-hands rule, and they will beg to be selected to throw the ball. Here is our best advice to avoid tears and temper tantrums: When your team is awarded a throw-in, shout out the name of someone who has not had an opportunity to throw the ball in recently. Try to choose someone in the general vicinity of the ball so as to not prolong the game. Just take turns. Eventually your players will get over the excitement of throwing the ball in, although it may not be until they are 10 or 11 years old; when this happens, simply teach them that the player closest to the ball throws it.

Although the quality of your team's throw-ins will not necessarily make or break your team's success at the recreational level, bad throw-ins still lead to turnovers. And turnovers can be costly, especially in your defensive half of the field. One bonus of throw-ins at this level is that players are often more accurate at throwing than they are at kicking. So be sure to set aside some practice time for this skill, or at least incorporate it in your scrimmages so your players have a chance to practice.

There are some rules for throwing the ball in properly. It is important that you go over these with your players, because the penalty for an improper throw-in is typically a throw-in for the opposing team. Check the league rules for your age group to find out if players get a second chance to throw the ball in or if the opposing team gets the ball. Here are the basic throw-in rules:

- Both feet must be touching the ground when the ball is released from the hands.
- Both feet must stay on or behind the sideline mark.
- The ball must go behind the head.
- Both hands must be used equally. In other words, a player cannot accidentally or purposefully add spin to the throw by using one hand more than the other.
- A goal cannot be scored directly from a throw-in. Someone must touch the ball (from either team) before it can go into the goal.
- If players break any of these rules, the referee may award the ball to the other team for a throw-in.

When first teaching players how to throw the ball, you may want to have them practice the technique without the ball. Have them go through the motions, help correct bad form, and then add the ball. This helps players focus on technique before they worry about the outcome of the throw. When you add balls, have enough balls for all the players (or at least half the players) to practice at the same time so the players can take lots of throws. You can use extra parents, a wall, or the goal to stop the rolling balls if you have all players throwing at the same time. Another option is to pair up players, and let them throw back and forth. With the second method, they can also practice receiving the ball from a throw-in.

To properly perform a throw-in, players stand a couple of steps back from the sideline. They hold the ball in their hands with the arms extended in front, gripping the sides of the ball in the middle. Fingers are comfortably spread apart so they have a solid handle on the ball. The fingers should be facing forward, and the thumbs should be facing up toward the sky. Players bend their elbows and move the ball behind the head so it almost touches the neck (see figure 8.3a). Instruct your players to bend their backs a little so that they throw the ball by moving the entire torso, not just the arms.

The player taking the throw-in must find the target and may even want to call the target's name. Taking a step toward the field, the thrower places both feet on the ground on the final step. The entire foot does not have to be on the ground. Typically the heel of the back foot will lift off the ground, leaving the toe touching the ground. As the player steps forward, she brings *both* hands over her head at the same time, keeping her eyes on the target. She keeps her body upright and releases the ball as it just passes over her head (figure 8.3*b*), snapping her wrists. The player then follows through toward the target.

You may see or hear other coaches teach their beginning soccer players to cross their feet when they throw in the ball in order to remind them to keep their feet on the ground. You are welcome to use this idea, but we have found that it just promotes incorrect technique. If your players are having a hard time keeping their feet on the ground, have them stand still (instead of taking a step) when they throw in the ball. Instead of yelling, "Keep your feet on the ground," tell them to imagine

Figure 8.3   For a throw-in, the player should grip the sides of the ball with both hands and (*a*) bring her arms back behind her head so that the ball almost touches her neck. The player then (*b*) brings the ball forward over her head and releases it when it is directly overhead.

their feet are glued to the ground. This is a fun image, and the kids can actually imagine how it feels, so it "sticks" with them.

Until your players are very comfortable throwing in the ball and receiving it well, encourage them to throw the ball down the field (toward your offensive half of the field) to a teammate, preferably an open teammate. If they are in their defensive half of the field, encourage them to throw the ball down the sideline. If they throw it into the center of the field, there is more opportunity for the opposing team to intercept the ball and take it to the goal. In the offensive half of the field, they can throw it either down the sideline or toward the goal. Typically a throw-in should be aimed at the feet of a teammate so it can be more easily controlled.

Heading

Using the head to direct the ball out of the air is an important part of the game of soccer, but it is not a skill that you need to spend a lot of time on during your season, especially if you are coaching younger children. Research is inconclusive on the long-term effects of excessive heading, but experts do recommend limiting the number of headers in a short period of time. A few headers during the game are fine, but an entire practice of heading is unnecessary and could be dangerous. It is important that you teach your players the correct way to use their heads so that if the head does come in contact with the ball, they know what to do and can actually reduce the risk of injury.

When something comes near our heads, our natural instinct is to duck, so don't expect your players to do any different at first. Picture a turtle pulling its head back into its shell. This will be a common image as your players learn the skill. And of course, if a turtle gets hit on the head as it is pulling back into the shell, it is going to hurt. Players who are timid when heading the ball will experience the same thing. Encourage your players to attack the ball rather than let it hit them; it will hurt a lot less if they head the ball rather than let it hit their heads. To reduce the number of sore heads that you hear your players complain about, be sure to teach them how to head the ball using the forehead.

To head a ball correctly, players should get their bodies behind the ball (see figure 8.4). The feet should be staggered and shoulder-width apart and the arms out to the side to protect them and help with balance. The arms shouldn't be extended like a scarecrow, but bent so the elbows are actually at the sides. Instruct players to keep their eyes on the ball and follow it as they make contact with it. Remind your players to keep their jaws closed. You do not want them to bite their tongues!

Players should arch their backs and swing their heads forward as the ball nears. Do not let them just bend their necks. Instruct players to keep their shoulders level and strike the ball as it arrives with the upper middle of the forehead. The goal is to make contact with the midpoint of the ball and send it forward down the field. Striking below the middle of the ball will make it rise. Striking above the midpoint will send it toward the ground. These steps are just for a basic header. Although diving headers and flicks are exciting to watch, focus on the basics for now. Getting these fundamentals down is the key to the other fancier headers.

Figure 8.4   Proper stance for heading a ball.

Drill 1 Partner Throws

Skill warm-up, skill training

EQUIPMENT
1 ball for every 2 players

PLAYING AREA
Enough room for players to stand about 5 yards (5 m) from their partners and at least 3 yards (3 m) away from the pair next to them

PURPOSE
Teaching proper throwing technique

PROCEDURE
Put players in pairs, and have each set of partners line up facing each other about 5 yards (5 m) apart. Players throw the ball back and forth to each other using the correct throwing technique. At first, you can let the players catch the throws, but eventually you should require them to receive the ball with their feet, thighs, or chests as they would in game play.

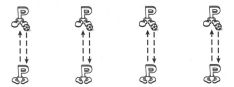

COACHING POINTS
Your players will want to jump as they throw the ball. Remind them to keep both feet on the ground as if they are stuck in glue.

MODIFICATIONS
Have the partner who is receiving the ball move away from the thrower and then back toward him as if he were getting rid of a defender before receiving a throw-in. This allows the thrower to practice throwing to a moving target.

Drill 2 Throw to Me

Skill warm-up, skill training

EQUIPMENT
1 ball for every 3 players

PLAYING AREA
The length of the sideline to 15 to 20 yards (14 to 18 m) out

PURPOSE
Teaching proper technique for throwing to a moving player

PROCEDURE
Organize players in groups of three. Spread the groups out along the sideline so each group has about 15 to 20 yards (14 to 18 m) to work in. Position player 1, who will throw in the ball, behind the sideline. The other

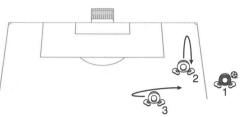

two teammates (player 2 and player 3) should be on the field preparing to receive the ball. Player 2 is positioned along the sideline. She should begin jogging down toward the attacking goal and then quickly turn and run back toward the thrower (this is a checking run). The player should call for the ball and be prepared to receive it at her feet. Player 3 is positioned toward the middle of the field. She should begin jogging toward the center of the field and then quickly turn and run back toward the thrower (another checking run). This player should also call for the ball and be prepared to receive it at her feet. Player 1 throws in the ball to player 2 or player 3. The player who receives the ball turns and dribbles a bit as if she is attacking the goal. Play then stops, the ball is knocked back to the thrower, and the process is repeated 9 more times. Players then switch roles and repeat the procedure, allowing everyone to practice throwing in the ball.

COACHING POINTS
Remind the players to bring the ball completely back over their heads so it is almost touching the neck.

MODIFICATIONS
Add a fourth player who is the defender. The defender should pick a player to mark and follow that player. The thrower should find the open player.

Drill 3 Heading Basics

Skill warm-up, skill training

EQUIPMENT
1 ball for every 2 players

PLAYING AREA
Area that gives players about 1 to 3 yards (1 to 3 m) between them

PURPOSE
Practicing proper heading technique

PROCEDURE
Players are in pairs. One player takes a seat on the ground, with knees bent and feet flat on the ground. A partner has the ball and is kneeling about 2 to 3 yards (2 to 3 m) away from her. The partner tosses the ball to the player on the ground, who rocks forward (as in a traditional sit-up) to head the ball back to the thrower, making contact with the ball at about the time the ball is moving over the player's abdomen. The player should make contact with the ball before completing the sit-up. Players repeat this procedure 10 times and then switch roles.

When both players have had a turn, the player on the ground moves to her knees. Again her partner tosses the ball to her. She leans her upper body back, rocks forward, and makes contact with the ball when it is still over her body (not out in front of her because power will be lost). She should follow through, letting her hands contact the ground in front of her. Players repeat this procedure 10 times and then switch roles.

MODIFICATIONS

When ready, players can move to a standing position and head the ball back to their partners. They can also practice heading the ball back and forth without using their hands. For safety, limit this activity to about 5 minutes.

Drill 4 PKs

Skill warm-up, skill training

EQUIPMENT
1 ball

PLAYING AREA
Penalty box on one end of the field

PURPOSE
Teaching penalty kicks (use only with age groups that use penalty kicks in games)

PROCEDURE
Allow each player to take one or two penalty kicks. Rotate goalkeepers in to defend the shots. A willing parent or sibling would be a good option here. After everyone has had at least one turn, begin an elimination game. Each player takes one penalty kick. If he scores, he stays in the game. If he misses, he is eliminated. Players who score move on to the second round, and they each take a second PK. Those who make that shot continue on to the next round. This continues until there is one player left who hasn't missed.

COACHING POINTS
Instruct the players to decide which corner of the goal they are going to aim for before approaching the ball and to shoot there. Remind them to strike the ball firmly, but not so hard that they sacrifice all accuracy.

MODIFICATIONS
Instead of elimination, divide the group into two even teams, and have a contest to see which team can score 5 PKs first. Or, allow the players to line up along the top of the box (like in a game) and then follow the kick if it is saved or hits a post.

Drill 5 Circle Heading

Skill training

EQUIPMENT
1 ball for every player

PLAYING AREA
10- to 15-yard (9 to 14 m) circle

PURPOSE
Teaching proper heading technique in a gamelike setting

PROCEDURE
Put players into groups of five or six. Form a circle with players around the circumference, and put one player in the middle. The players on the outside (the throwers) should each have a ball. The player in the middle (the header) faces a player on the outside, calls his name, and prepares for a toss. The thrower tosses the ball to the header, who heads it back to him. The header repeats this procedure for eight randomly selected throws. (The throws

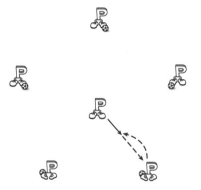

should *not* move in order around the circle.) Then, the header switches places with a thrower, and the new header repeats the task.

COACHING POINTS
Remember, some debate exists about the safety of excess heading. Practicing heading is important so your players can learn the correct technique, but limit the sessions to about 10 minutes total, allowing players to take only one or two turns in the middle of the circle. Be sure that players keep their eyes open and focused on the ball during the approach, when making contact, and after the ball has been headed. Watch to make sure they head the ball with the middle to upper part of the forehead and make contact with the middle of the ball.

MODIFICATIONS
Add a defender to the inside of the circle whose job is to challenge the header.

Drill 6 Goal Clearances

Skill training

EQUIPMENT
1 ball for every 2 players

PLAYING AREA
Half the field

PURPOSE
Practicing using the proper technique when taking goal kicks

PROCEDURE
Pair players and have them line up facing each other, 10 yards (9 m) apart. Have them pass the ball back and forth using the inside-of-the-foot pass. As they begin to warm up, have them spread farther apart and begin using the driven pass technique. When the pair is 30 to 50 yards (27 to 46 m) apart, have them drive a stationary ball back and forth to simulate the goal kick. Practicing driving a stationary ball is important because the ball for a goal kick won't be moving as they approach it.

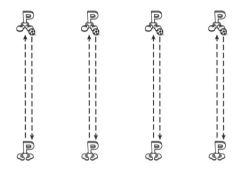

Drill 7 Finding a Target

Skill training

EQUIPMENT
Two balls (only 1 ball is used for each group at a time)

PLAYING AREA
Half the field

PURPOSE
Teaching finding an open player or open space with a goal kick

PROCEDURE
Make sure players have warmed up using the driven pass or crossing technique. Split the players into two groups. One group will work on the right side of the goal while the other group will work on the left side of the goal. Select three or four players who may take goal kicks, and keep those players stationed down by the

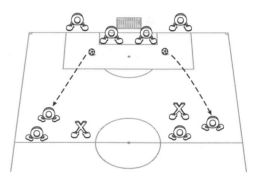

goal. The other players spread out just short of midfield. Designate one out of every three players at midfield to be the opposition. So, if you have six players spread out at midfield, four are on the same team as the players taking the goal kicks and two are on the other team. They are trying to challenge the goal kick team. The players by the goal will practice taking goal kicks and finding a target (one of their teammates). Require the target players to move around preparing to receive the ball. The players taking goal kicks get a point when they successfully hit a target with a solid goal kick. Targets get a point if they move in preparation to receive the ball and then handle it under control. Play to 5 or 6 points, then rotate the players so others get to be the opposition.

COACHING POINTS
Encourage the players taking the goal kicks to find a target who is on the side of the field the ball is on. Instruct the target players to move toward the ball, and when they receive it, to get it under control as quickly as possible.

Drill 8 Basic Corner

Skill training, team training

EQUIPMENT
1 ball; pinnies

PLAYING AREA
Area in front of the goal

PURPOSE
Teaching taking basic corner kicks, making effective runs, and preparing to receive the ball

PROCEDURE
Set the team up as if they are on offense, getting ready to take a corner kick. A kicker, who will cross the ball in front of the goal, starts at the corner with a ball. Three offensive players are positioned together near the top of the goal box, preparing to run toward the goal. Use extra players as defenders trying to stop the play.

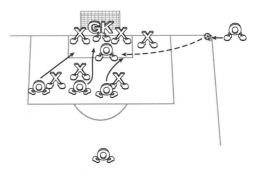

Remember to keep one or two players back to defend a counterattack. As the kicker approaches the ball, the offensive players in front of the goal make different runs. One player runs toward the near post (closest to the ball), one runs toward the far post, and one runs toward the middle of the goal. Other offensive players should be positioned around the box to help keep the ball in that end of the field if the defense tries to clear it out. Repeat the play several times. Consider having more than one player attempt the kicks. If they are able, the kickers should send some kicks to the near side of the goal and some across to the far post.

COACHING POINTS
Each runner should use changes in speed and direction to create space from the defenders. Be sure the runners time their runs so they are still moving when the ball arrives at the area in front of the goal. The runner in position to receive the cross should work to position his run so it intersects the path of the ball. The runners who do not receive the cross should frame the goal and follow the shot.

MODIFICATIONS
Set the team up to defend a corner kick and focus on defensive points, such as marking an opponent, moving to the ball, and solid clearing of the ball.

Drill 9 Short Corner

Skill training, team training

EQUIPMENT
1 ball; pinnies

PLAYING AREA
Area in front of the goal

PURPOSE
Teaching short corner kicks

PROCEDURE
Set up for an offensive corner kick, using extra players as defenders. Have two players set up at the corner with the ball. Rather than cross it into the area in front of the goal, player 1 approaches the ball and passes it to player 2. As the defense shifts toward the ball, player 2 has the option of crossing it or passing it back to player 1. If player 2 passes the ball, player 1 should then look to cross it in front of the goal. The other offensive players should make runs in front of the goal preparing to receive the ball from either teammate. If they make a run and the ball is not crossed in, they can circle back and make a similar run again.

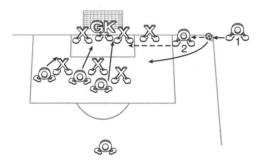

COACHING POINTS
Remind the players to watch the defense and take advantage if they cheat toward the ball. Instruct the runners in front of the goal to delay their runs until just before the ball is crossed. Instruct the runners in front of the goal to make additional runs if the ball isn't sent in the first time. Teach players to use change of speed and change of direction to escape the defenders and create space. Remind players to cross the ball before the opponent has a chance to apply too much pressure.

MODIFICATIONS
Encourage player 2 in the corner to dribble in toward the goal and take a shot if there is an opening.

Drill 10 Basic Free Kicks

Skill training, team training

EQUIPMENT
1 ball; pinnies

PLAYING AREA
Half the field, including the area in front of a goal

PURPOSE
Teaching direct and indirect free kicks

PROCEDURE
Set up one team on offense, and use the remaining players as defenders. Slowly walk the players through the basic free kick formation provided in this chapter on page 173. One or two players should stay back to defend a counterattack, one or two players should line up at the ball, and the other players

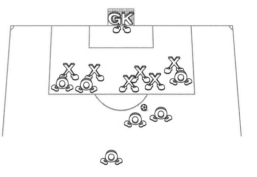

should prepare to follow the shot. Then randomly move the ball around the area in front of the goal and call fouls. For example, say, "Direct kick for pushing," or "Indirect kick for dangerous play," and help the players quickly move into position to take the kick. On a direct kick, the shooter can just hit the ball. If it is an indirect kick, one player should pass the ball (or at least tap the ball) before the shooter takes the shot. Allow the players to switch roles so most of them get to be shooters, followers (garbagemen), or defenders.

COACHING POINTS
Shooters should focus on keeping the ball in play and trying to get a good shot on goal. Followers focus on reading the play and anticipating an opportunity to follow a shot, save, or deflection. Remind players that two people must touch the ball before it goes in the goal on an indirect free kick.

MODIFICATIONS
Move the goals close to each other to create a very short field. Divide the players into two even teams. Scrimmage, but frequently call fouls (make them up if you have to) so each team practices offensive and defensive free kicks. You can use this drill for any formation that you might want to use with your team.

The Coach's Clipboard

✔ With each stoppage of play, there is an accompanying restart.

✔ When the ball goes out of bounds on the side of the field, play is restarted with a throw-in.

✔ If the ball goes over the end line from the defensive team, a corner kick is awarded.

✔ If the ball goes over the end line from the offensive team, a goal kick is awarded.

✔ Free kicks are restarts that take place after a foul or violation of the rules.

✔ A kickoff is used to start the game, each half (or quarter), and after a goal has been scored.

✔ When designing restart plays, remember to keep it simple, Supercoach.

✔ Design your restart strategies around creating a scoring opportunity, maintaining possession, or getting the ball down the field.

✔ When heading the ball, players should use the forehead and attack the ball rather than let it hit them.

Formations and Team Play Basics

reating a successful youth soccer team is a lot like building a house. You need people who can take on specific roles yet work together toward a common goal. You need to be able to express your wants and needs and know that the workers are listening. The workers must be able to communicate effectively with one another as well. The plan and the work must be organized, and everyone must work in unison if the project is going to stay on track. Luckily, it is often easier to motivate players than contractors because players have a large stake in the outcome of their work.

Basic Principles of Team Play

As you take your players through their dribbling, passing, and shooting drills, you also need to begin molding them into a team. There are certain principles you should introduce so that the players can make the most of the skills they are learning, but keep in mind that younger players will grasp, at best, only the most basic tactical principles. Encourage the kids to work together to defend, to move the ball down the field, and to create goal-scoring opportunities. There are five basic principles of team play:

1. Shape
2. Support
3. Communication
4. Moving as a team
5. Possession

Shape

One of the most challenging principles to teach is team shape. Although soccer players can go anywhere on the field, it is still important that the team have some set formation. Your players should be positioned on the field in a manner so there is both width and depth. Specific formations are discussed later in the chapter, but the basic idea is to have a goalkeeper (if used in your age group), defenders, midfielders, and forwards. Those players should be spaced out so they can use every area of the field. It is perfectly appropriate to tell players where they will typically be positioned on the field, but try not to limit their movement completely.

Team shape is a concept that can be shown on a whiteboard, on a handout, or by using players or cones at practice. Consider positioning players during some drills so they are forced to provide width and depth and maintain their shape. Stop play during scrimmages to point out effective team shape or to help players figure out where to move to maintain their shape. Some analogies you can use when emphasizing the shortcomings of a soccer team with poor shape are a two-legged stool, a raft that's not inflated, or a puzzle with missing pieces. However you choose to explain, the principles of team shape are worth covering during practice.

Support

One of the reasons that soccer is the most popular sport in the world is that it is a true team sport, in the purest sense. The size of the field, the length of the game, and the nature of the sport dictate that success is determined far more often by the ability of the team than by each individual player. The word we use for how players help one another both offensively and defensively is *support*. This is a fundamental principle of team play. There are three types of support that you should coach your players to incorporate in their play. Two of these involve actual tactical concepts: offensive support and defensive support. The other type of support is the emotional encouragement players should exhibit toward their teammates.

Offensively, players support their teammates by making themselves available to receive the ball. This means moving into open space and running into passing lanes. The goal is to make it as easy as possible for the player with the ball to find an open teammate. Whenever a player has the ball at his feet, there should be a teammate supporting him from behind, a teammate moving out to the side, and a teammate making a run into open space in front. Players moving without the ball have two jobs. One is to get open by freeing themselves from defenders. The other job is to create space for the player with the ball. Sometimes the best thing a teammate can do is check away from the player with the ball with the goal of bringing a defender with her.

Support on defense requires all players to do their jobs. Whether the team is marking man-to-man or playing more of a zone defense, everyone must work to stay on the same page. While working to cover a mark or an area, each player must also be watching for opportunities to support his teammates. The second defender in particular plays this role, but other defenders can help out as well. Defensive support means working to move into position to support the teammate or teammates trying to immediately stop an attack. The guidelines that follow can help you teach players to provide defensive support. If you become frustrated that your players aren't getting it, be patient. This is a tricky concept.

- Players should get behind the ball. They should move to be between the ball and the goal.
- Players need to move to positions where they can help their team-mates while still maintaining responsibility for their mark or their area of the field.
- Players must communicate with their teammates.
- Solid defense takes hard work. The harder a team works together, the more effective the players will be as a defensive unit.

When it's time to work on your team's emotional support, don't panic. This doesn't mean holding hands, hugging, and buying tissues. Emotional support simply means maintaining positive morale when the team is play-ing well and also when the team is struggling. Encourage the players to communicate positively: "Good try," "Good hustle," "Nice going," "You'll get the next one." Simple acts like high-fiving and helping a player up when she falls or gets knocked down can generate positive, supportive interaction among teammates. As a coach, you can encourage this support when you lead by example. Look for opportunities to praise the players, and find good in their effort and willingness to take risks, even when they make mistakes.

Communication

Continually stress to your players the importance of communication. To work well together, any group of people must be able to talk and listen. Players should communicate with one another about what is happening on the field. They should help direct the player with the ball to an open teammate. Players without the ball should help one another move into open space and communicate with each other about the defenders.

Your players should also communicate about strengths, weaknesses, and tendencies of the other team. If a player notices that the other team is dribbling more than passing, he should mention this to his teammates and tell them to pressure the ball and move to support the first defender. If a midfielder realizes that she is much faster than the player trying to defend her, she should tell her offensive teammates that she has a favorable matchup. Encourage your players to talk about what is happening on the field. This will help them analyze and process the game, and ultimately this will help them become smarter soccer players.

Communication on the field must be practiced like any other skill. Make sure the players learn and then use each other's names, starting with the very first practice. During even the most basic drills, players should call one another by name when passing or receiving the ball. While working within small games or drills where players have options, require them to pass the ball only to a teammate who calls for it by name. Drills and practice scenarios are less intense and less stressful than the actual game. Players must be able to communicate effectively in this environment if they are going to carry it over into an actual match.

As the players' ability to effectively communicate on the field progresses, emphasize two key points: (1) Listening is as important as talking, and (2) effective communication is easily processed by the person on the receiving end. As the coach watching and evaluating the play, watch for players who are not only talking but also listening and responding. It doesn't do any good for Joe to say, "Man on, Derek," if Derek ignores him and tries to turn with the ball anyway. Players must work to listen for what is being said and to understand how to best use that information.

Brief, clear directions are much easier to take in and decipher than vague cues or long sentences. The most common communication breakdown occurs when one player has the ball and every one of her teammates wants it and is screaming her name, whether or not they are open. So here is Makenzie dribbling down the field, and she can hear her name being called in front of her, behind her, and to both sides. But she doesn't know who the best option is, and she doesn't have time to check all of them.

To be more effective, the player behind Makenzie could be telling her that she has time or that Sydney is open wide right. The player in front could say, "Play my feet," or "Send it into space," so Makenzie doesn't have to guess where to play the ball. Practice effective communication during the week so the kids are ready to talk and listen on Saturday morning. You may need to give the players some simple words and phrases they can use to communicate clearly. You don't need a code, just some basic cues that always mean the same thing. Here are a few examples:

- Man on—There is a defender very close; you may need to protect or get rid of the ball quickly.
- Back—Drop the ball back to me.
- Right or Left—Directs the dribbler to the right or left.
- Inside or Outside—Directs the dribbler to the inside or outside.
- Cross—Send the ball into the middle from the outside.
- Step—Pressure the ball immediately.
- Clear or Out—Send the ball up the field immediately.
- Turn—Turn with the ball to go another way.
- Time—You have time and space to control the ball.
- Down the line—Pass the ball down the sideline.

Moving as a Team

To maintain shape and stay organized on the field, the team must move together. At times, especially when on defense, this means players moving as if they were all connected. A common mistake is for defenders to line up at the top of their own penalty box and stay there regardless of where the ball is on the field. When their team has the ball, these players should be supporting the play and moving down the field. They will generally remain behind the midfielders, and they probably won't find themselves very far across the half line, but they should continue to move when their team is in possession of the ball.

Imagine your team as the players on foosball rods. Aside from being able to spin them to help them kick the ball harder, you would also be able to move them in unison. As the right defender moves out toward the sideline, the central defender would shift out to the right and the left defender would move toward the middle of the field. Ideally, your team should shift in this manner. The downside of foosball as a metaphor is that the players are in flat lines across the field. In reality, this approach would leave your team vulnerable to balls being played between defenders. Along with their movement together from side to side, your team needs to shift together forward and backward. When the opposition is attacking with the ball, all the players should be shifting back toward their own goal. This doesn't mean that all players must sprint back to the penalty box, but they should move in that direction while maintaining the team's shape. When the team is on offense, the midfielders should move downfield to help the forwards. At the same time, the defenders should stay in position to support the midfielders.

Offensively, there should be some shifting together to help ensure that the player with the ball always has help. However, a lot of offensive movement is dictated by openings created by the other team. Moving together offensively means supporting the player with the ball, moving to create space for the player with the ball, and moving to create space for other teammates to attack. During practice, coach the players to move away from the ball first and then check to the ball quickly. The idea is for the player to distance himself from a defender. Build on this idea by encouraging another player to move into the space that the checking player left. Each time a player runs into space, he is also leaving a space that a teammate should then occupy. When the team is on offense, players should be constantly in motion, watching and working to move along with their teammates.

Possession

You may have heard the saying that possession is nine-tenths of the law. That may or may not be true, but possession is the key to winning in most sports. Almost all goals scored in soccer are scored by the offensive team. Thus, it stands to reason that you want your team to have and keep possession of the ball. You may direct your players to attack and move the ball down the field very quickly. This type of offense is often referred to as a direct style of play. Or you may coach your players to move the ball around the field, creating openings in the opposing defense before ultimately initiating an attack. Different teams and different circumstances may require a different approach. Those decisions are based on the skill level of your team and the skill level of your opponent. However, the concept of possession remains the same. You want your team to have the ball more than the other team has the ball.

Keeping possession of the ball requires players to stay organized, move into open space, and pass the ball accurately and purposefully. Start with quality technical sessions where the focus is on passing and receiving the ball. Build on these passing drills by incorporating communication and movement. Slowly increase intensity by adding a defender or restricting the amount of space the players have to move within. You can also challenge the players by restricting the number of consecutive touches each player can take on the ball before passing it to a teammate.

A very popular practice game at all levels of soccer is 5v2 in which five offensive players work to keep the ball away from two defenders inside a circle or square grid. A wide variety of technical and tactical points can be emphasized in this game. One point that is often neglected when focusing on team possession is transition, which is the instant a team switches from defense to offense or offense to defense. A team that is slow in transition typically struggles to get organized and may allow the other team to gain a decided advantage in the play. A team that is fast in transition can take advantage of holes and weaknesses in the opposition.

When your team wins the ball, each player should quickly look to support the player who has the ball and then move into open spaces where a pass might be received. During that transition, there may be openings left by players from the other team who weren't prepared to defend. Those players may have made runs hoping to get the ball and are now out of position or unaware of their mark. Coach your players to look for those openings and communicate quickly to get into those spaces. Transitioning quickly after losing possession of the ball is also important. Emphasize to your players that they must get back behind the ball and find open players to mark as quickly as possible.

Formations and Systems

You may have only four or five practices with your team before games start, or in some cases even less than that. Regardless of the number of practices, you will still think your team has a lot more to learn before you can start playing. You should focus on coaching the basic skills first. However, it is a team sport, so you have to address that aspect in some fashion. In preparing for the first game, some coaches simply throw their players out onto the field and let them figure it out. This is probably not your best option, but obsessing about the details of your team formation is not productive either. Ideally, you will introduce some ideas about formation, so your team will be organized at least at the kickoff.

Soccer formations are also referred to as systems of play. Either term means the number of players you have in each of the three basic groups of positions: defenders, midfielders, and forwards. If your age group plays with only three to seven players on the field for each team, sometimes only two groups of positions are used: defenders and forwards. The name of any formation identifies the number of players in the defenders, midfielders, and forwards group, in that order.

For example, if the league requires your team's age group to play with eight players, including a goalkeeper, and you have three defenders, three midfielders, and one forward, then you are playing a 3-3-1. You do not include the goalkeeper in the line because the positioning of that player does not change between formations. If you play with three players in one group of positions, you will typically have a central player and two outside players in that group. If you play with two players in a given group, bring them closer to the center of the field so they can work together and cover the middle of the field.

Choose a formation that fits your players' abilities. Do not get sucked in by the desire to look organized and force your players into a specific formation. Also, do not force players into a single position. You should rotate players not only from game to game but within a game as well. Specialization is for elite players and not for beginners. Help your players develop all aspects of their game by challenging them in different situations as the season goes on. However, for the first couple of games, it is okay to start players in positions where they are most comfortable. As you teach them new skills, you can encourage them to take risks and try new positions. You can use the following descriptions to match players to positions, but, remember, these are only guidelines. They are not hard and fast rules, and these characteristics should not relegate a player to one position all season.

- Defenders—larger, strong, persistent, scrappy, physical, willing to accept role
- Midfielders—solid foot skills and awareness, quick, mobile, experienced
- Forwards—fast, aggressive, slightly selfish, creative

Discussing all the possible formations you can use is not practical because the number of players on the field varies by age and league. In addition, formations should be developed around players instead of forcing players into a specific system. For these reasons, this section provides general guidelines for formations based on the number of players on the field.

Formations for Playing Without Goalkeepers

For coaches who are working with U6 and U8 teams and other age groups that play with fewer than five players, focus on staggering your players when positioning them on the field. In other words, you want someone slightly in front of and someone slightly behind the person with the ball (see figure 9.1). The players should not be in a straight line but more of a triangle shape. This gives you some offense with a little defensive protection. Triangles allow for depth (forward and back) and width (right and left) among players. But let's be realistic—these young players who are new to the game will chaotically move around the field, more in an amoeba shape than a triangle, at least until you get your hands on them for a season or two! The idea of triangles promotes sharing (passing), which is one of the main goals with this age group. When on defense, focus on pressure, cover, and balance (first, second, and third defenders).

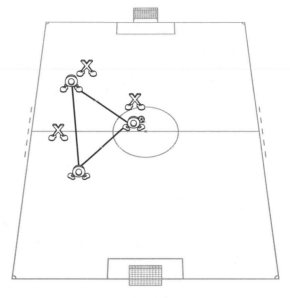

Figure 9.1   A triangle formation.

With four players on the field, the best formation is a diamond shape for both offense and defense (see figure 9.2). With this formation, one player (your main defender) provides depth, and two players provide width—one positioned toward each sideline. This leaves one player (your primary attacker) providing length. This formation allows for players to learn the importance of moving as a team. Because the diamond is essentially two triangles base-to-base, players can easily provide and receive support.

Another possible formation with four players on the field is to have two defenders and two attackers, creating more of a square. With this formation, however, it is easy for players to fall into

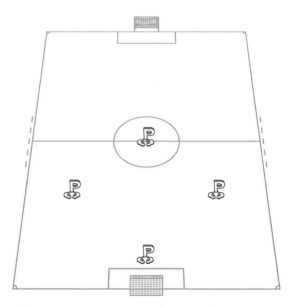

Figure 9.2   A diamond formation with four players.

the trap of working only as defenders or attackers. The diamond shape is more conducive for team development, and it opens up the field of play because the center is open for players to move in and out of that area.

Formations With Goalkeepers and Fewer Than Seven Field Players

By the time players reach the U10 age group (which usually has five or six players on the field for each team plus the goalkeepers), they are able to understand the basic aspects of the game. They are more comfortable with sharing the ball and understanding their positional roles. Three groups of positions may still be too complicated, so a 3-2 or 3-3 formation may be the easiest to implement. These formations have three defenders and two or three forwards, depending on the total number of field players. Players can easily understand their main role and secondary role as well as what space they are supposed to cover.

With three defenders, there will be one central defender and two outside defenders (known as outside backs), one on the right and one on the left. This backline of defenders can be set up in two different ways. One option is to place the defenders in a V shape as shown in figure 9.3, with the center player deeper than the outside players. The deep central player is in front of the goalkeeper but behind all her teammates. This player is known as the sweeper because she sweeps the loose balls and cleans up the back part of the field as the last line of defense. While the central player sweeps the field, the outside defenders provide first-defender pressure and second-defender support when the opponent is attacking. When the team is on offense, the outside defenders should move up the field, offering support to the forwards.

Another option is to have the three defenders in a line like the Nike swoosh, often called a flat back three (see figure 9.4) or flat back four. Interestingly, the flat back defense is not really flat. It is called *flat* in the soccer world because no single player is solely responsible for being the last defender. This defensive shape is flatter than the V defensive

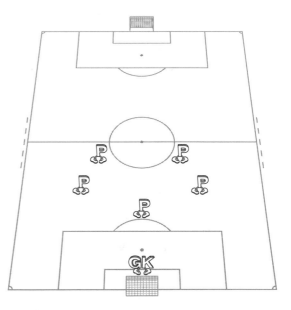

Figure 9.3 Placement at kickoff for a 3-2 formation with three defenders in a V shape and two attackers in front.

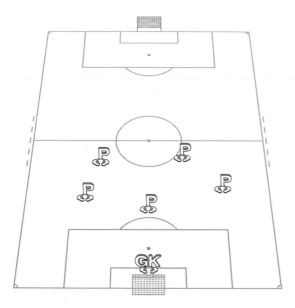

Figure 9.4   Placement at kickoff for a 3-2 formation with three defenders in a flat back position and two attackers in front.

shape with the sweeper, so think of it as *flatter* back three. More specifically, the shape of the defenders in the flat back changes relative to the location of the ball, with the defender closest to the ball serving as the first defender. The next closest defender is the second defender, and the third defender provides balance on the fields (so one side of the field is not completely open).

Regardless of the arrangements of the defenders, you now want to think about your forwards. If you have two forwards, designate one as the right forward and one as the left forward. With only two of them, they will play more toward the center of the field. If the two forwards are positioned too far wide, a huge gap is created in the middle of the field. This space is easy for the opposing team to control. The forwards must support one another by providing a passing option at all times. As a rule of thumb, encourage them to be within about 5 to 10 yards (5 to 9 m) of each other (depending on the size of the field), moving together as if a rope were tied between them. Even though they are assigned to the right or left side, these two players should be encouraged to make runs when they see open space or an opportunity to win a ball, even when this means they switch sides of the field.

If you play with three forwards, you will have a right outside, a left outside, and a central forward. The outside players should stay wide on offense, almost all the way to the sideline. The goals of the central player are to get the ball wide to a teammate and then move toward the player to provide a passing option. When the team is defending, outside forwards should slide more central, closing down the space in the middle of the field. All the players should move up the field together when attacking and recover toward the back line to provide extra defensive pressure when the other team has the ball.

Formations With Eight or More Players

At the U12 level, teams typically play with seven players and a goal-keeper, which is more like the full-sided game of 11v11 when it comes to formations. There are more formation options, and more organization is needed to be successful. Assess your team's strengths and weak-nesses, and then decide what formation might be appropriate. It is okay to change your mind as the season progresses. You don't have to stick with one formation for the entire season. It is nice for your players to be comfortable with more than just one formation, although it may be challenging for them if you are teaching them a new formation every week. Regardless of your formation choice, you will need to make the following decisions when selecting a formation:

- **Will you play with a sweeper or a flat back system?** This important decision will be influenced by the number of defenders you have. If you have several smart, quick defenders, you may want to play with a flat back because they may be able to grasp the idea of pressure, cover, and balance as well as catch speedy opponents. On the other hand, if you have one really solid defender but few other defenders with much experience, or if you have several solid defenders who lack speed, you may want to play with a sweeper. The sweeper formation does not take as much team organization and field awareness as the flat back. If you have fewer experienced players, it might be overwhelming to have them shift across the field and change their shape to reflect the opponent's movement. They may be looking for concrete positions and roles; the sweeper formation offers this.

- **Do you need to emphasize a solid defensive system?** There are many reasons why you might decide to go with a more defensive system. You may have players with limited goalkeeping experience, so you want to limit the pressure on the goalkeeper by providing extra defensive support. You may have an inexperienced team, so you need to play conservatively. Whatever the reason, if you believe you need to play with a solid defensive system, you may want to play a 3-3-1 (see figure 9.5) or a 3-2-2 (see figure 9.6). These for-mations provide three defenders and at least two midfielders who can provide defensive help. If you decide to focus on defense, you will sacrifice your offensive opportunities; just decide if this is a sacrifice you need to make. The 3-2-2 allows for a solid defense but still some offensive power.

Figure 9.5 A 3-3-1 formation at kickoff includes a left back (LB), center back (CB), right back (RB), left midfielder (LM), center midfielder (CM), right midfielder (RM), and forward (F).

Figure 9.6 A 3-2-2 formation at kickoff includes a left back (LB), center back (CB), right back (RB), left midfielder (LM), right midfielder (RM), left forward (LF), and right forward (RF).

- **Can you afford to take some risks and go with a more offensive system?** If you think you have solid players in the back and can afford to push more players forward, you may select a 2-3-2 formation (see figure 9.7). With this formation, you place two solid players in the back, three players in the midfield (with the most talented player in the center midfield), and then two forwards up front. With five players able to attack the opposing goal, the players should have many options for passes, and a player should always be able to attack the goal and follow shots.

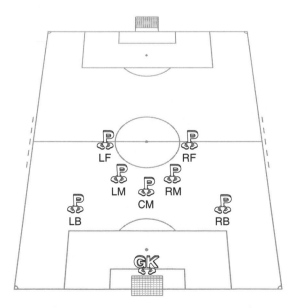

Figure 9.7 A 2-3-2 formation at kickoff includes a left back (LB), right back (RB), left midfielder (LM), center midfielder (CM), right midfielder (RM), left forward (LF), and right forward (RF).

Teaching the Formations

When teaching players about formations of play, it is helpful to first provide a diagram of what you want the team to look like. You can draw a soccer field on a piece of paper or whiteboard and use Xs to represent the location of players. Or in a small area on the field, arrange your cones to represent positions. Kids are very visual learners, so be sure to provide them with a diagram of some sort. You should also discuss the goals of the formation, the roles of each individual position, how each individual position fits into the team's big picture, and where players might play. Be as concrete and simple as possible. Focus most of your time on the role of each position.

After you have discussed formations with your players and reviewed their individual roles and the goals of the team, place players on the field in their assigned positions, relative to where they would stand during a kickoff. Let them see how the team should look and explore their space and distance from other players. On game day, remind players about the formation, and let them take their appropriate places during restarts.

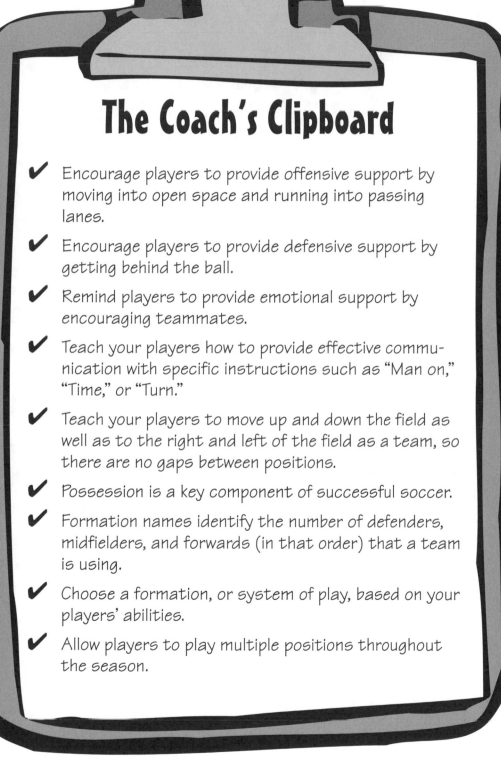

The Coach's Clipboard

✔ Encourage players to provide offensive support by moving into open space and running into passing lanes.

✔ Encourage players to provide defensive support by getting behind the ball.

✔ Remind players to provide emotional support by encouraging teammates.

✔ Teach your players how to provide effective communication with specific instructions such as "Man on," "Time," or "Turn."

✔ Teach your players to move up and down the field as well as to the right and left of the field as a team, so there are no gaps between positions.

✔ Possession is a key component of successful soccer.

✔ Formation names identify the number of defenders, midfielders, and forwards (in that order) that a team is using.

✔ Choose a formation, or system of play, based on your players' abilities.

✔ Allow players to play multiple positions throughout the season.

Game Time!
What's My Role Again?

Mrs. Carpenter is busy cutting oranges and putting drink boxes on ice. Your players have been wearing their uniforms, including shin guards, since the minute they woke up. And there might just be a couple of butterflies starting to stir in your stomach. That can mean only one thing. It's the best day of the week—game day. This, Coach, is your opportunity to see how well you've done with your practices. For your players, it's a chance to put on the uniform and play. No more drills; no more practice games against their own teammates. This is for real.

Planning Playing Time

Planning playing time is a part of the coach's job that must be thought through before the game. If you try to just wing it and make adjustments and substitutions throughout the game, many problems could arise. If you have more than one player to substitute, it will be hard to stay organized without a plan or system in place. Over the course of the season, each player should have a chance to play most positions. This task is easier to manage if you are organized. In the event that a parent expresses concern about his child's playing time or positioning on the field, you can respond more effectively if you can share your plan or philosophy with him. For all these reasons, a little planning up front can save you multiple headaches throughout the season.

Managing playing time can be challenging at the younger age groups. At this level, the main emphasis is participation and an introduction to the basic skills and concepts of soccer. The skills, tactics, and intensity level will obviously increase from the 5-year-olds to the 10-year-olds, but the main idea is still that the kids are playing soccer and having fun. Your challenge is to balance playing time, fun, and at least a little bit of learning. Two guiding principles should determine playing time: (1) any rules or guidelines set by your league and (2) the philosophy by which you are coaching this team.

The first principle is pretty clear. Many leagues have playing-time guidelines that coaches must adhere to, such as the following:

- Each player must participate in each half of the game.
- Each player must play at least half of the game.
- A player may play a maximum of one half in goal.
- Each player on a given team must start a game during the season.

Be sure to read your league's playing-time rules well before the first game. It may be a good idea to explain them to the parents and players so they understand what restrictions are in place.

The second principle ensures that how you manage playing time is clear and consistent with your coaching philosophy. In the younger age groups, especially, participation is priority number one. That means playing time should be fairly equal, and each player should have the opportunity to start some games throughout the season. It isn't necessary to count minutes for each player, and they won't all get the same time each game. If a couple of players get lots of time one game, then maybe they get a bit less during the next match.

You can use the playing-time record sheet in figure 10.1 (or create your own) to help you keep track of playing time. Make several copies of this sheet, and use one for each game. We recommend penciling in ideas of who is going to play each period before you arrive at the field. Then during the game, you (or an assigned parent) can mark in pen which players actually played during each period. You can also mark their position (D = defender, M = midfielder, and F = forward) if this is appropriate for your team's age group. Keep these sheets, as well as your starting lineups from each match, in your team notebook so you have all the information on hand when you need it.

Keep in mind that you are dealing with young children, so your plans are likely to be interrupted. Jessica will be late the day you have her starting up front. Just after being subbed in for Ricky, Marcus will throw up the candy bar he ate on the way to the field, and Stephanie will definitely

Figure 10.1 Playing-Time Record Sheet

Date: _____

Opponent: _____

Player	Period 1	Period 2	Period 3	Period 4

S = player started the period; P = player substituted into the period; D = played defense; M = played midfield; F = played forward

From L. Blom and T. Blom, 2009, *Survival Guide for Coaching Youth Soccer* (Champaign, IL: Human Kinetics).

get hit in the stomach with the ball moments after being put in goal. Plan for everything you can control, and expect lots of other things to come up along the way. Be prepared to be flexible. Remember, patience and persistence will get you through it!

Defining Your Role

As we have said before, soccer is a player's game. There is a reason there aren't any time-outs and, at the higher levels, the only stoppage in play is halftime. Almost all instruction should take place during practice. On game day, the coach is essentially responsible for setting an example, maintaining order, and helping the kids have fun.

The social atmosphere of a youth soccer game should always remain positive. As the coach, you have a tremendous opportunity to set the tone for the players, parents, fans, and even the opposing team. You serve as a role model for all these groups. If you yell and argue with the referees, the players and parents will follow suit. If you scream at the players and throw your clipboard, expect to have players yelling at one another on the field and throwing tantrums when something doesn't go their way. Remember that you don't have the luxury of just being an individual spectator at the event. You are a coach. Even if you aren't a soccer expert, you have stepped up to the challenge and taken on a leadership role. How you carry yourself on game day will influence the attitudes and behaviors of the participants and spectators.

Another of your responsibilities is to provide mature adult supervision. You should arrive at the field early and be prepared to stay after the game until all the players have been picked up by their parents. Once the players are at the field, they are ultimately your responsibility. It is your place to ensure they are behaving appropriately. Don't allow your players to run all over the complex, disrupt other teams that are playing or warming up, or goof off at the concession stand or in restroom areas. If you run into a major discipline problem, ask a parent or another league official for help so that you can focus your attention on the rest of the team.

Managing Pregame Details

On the big day, you want to make sure you have the equipment your team needs and that you have completed the pregame tasks. Depending on the league requirements and the age group you are coaching, the equipment and tasks may vary. Figure 10.2 is an equipment checklist to you can use to ensure that you bring everything you and your team will need. Adjust it to fit your situation.

Once you arrive at the field, you have a few pregame tasks as a coach. Figure 10.3 lists the steps you will need to complete to get ready for the game. Again, feel free to adjust it to fit your team's situation. The two main areas of pregame details relate to playing conditions and player preparation. In regard to the playing conditions, you should check that the goals are in place and make sure that nothing has been left on the field that might present a hazard to the players. Kids have a right to participate in recreational sports in a safe and healthy environment. This means there is a safe distance between the sidelines and any benches, bleachers, fences, or posts. It also means that the field the kids are playing on is free

Figure 10.2 Equipment Checklist

Before you leave your house, make sure you have the following items:

- ❑ Soccer balls for warm-up
- ❑ A game ball (if required to be supplied by the coach)
- ❑ A few cones
- ❑ Coaching attire (your team shirt with "Coach" on the back or other comfortable clothes)
- ❑ Your tennis shoes or cleats
- ❑ An extra pair of socks for the player who forgot them
- ❑ An extra pair of shin guards (you never know when your star player will forget these)
- ❑ Team goalkeeper gloves (if your team plays with a goalkeeper)
- ❑ Sheet with ideas about who will play where and in which quarter and half
- ❑ Team notebook
- ❑ Halftime snacks (or know who is scheduled to bring them)
- ❑ Postgame refreshments (or know who is scheduled to bring them)
- ❑ Bottle of water (or a water jug) for you
- ❑ Extra water for your players (or know who is scheduled to bring this)
- ❑ Weather-appropriate items (e.g. rain jacket, sunscreen, hat, sweatshirt)
- ❑ First aid kit
- ❑ Cell phone
- ❑ Roster (in case you have not learned everyone's name or need to contact someone)
- ❑ Medical forms and/or emergency contact information for your players
- ❑ Other _____
- ❑ Other _____
- ❑ Other _____

From L. Blom and T. Blom, 2009, *Survival Guide for Coaching Youth Soccer* (Champaign, IL: Human Kinetics).

Figure 10.3 Pregame Tasks

Before the game starts, be sure to complete the following tasks:

- ❑ Greet each player.
- ❑ Check the playing surface to make sure everything looks safe (there are no big rocks, the goals are weighted down, trash is removed, and so on).
- ❑ Make sure each player has the necessary equipment and it is properly fitted.
- ❑ Check with parents about halftime and postgame refreshments (if no one brought them, someone can run out and pick up snacks).
- ❑ Greet the officials.
- ❑ Lead players through a warm-up.
- ❑ Give the team one to three specific technical or tactical instructions for the game.
- ❑ Take a bathroom trip (for you or the players!).
- ❑ Give the team time to say their team cheer or prayer.
- ❑ Share the starting lineup with the team.
- ❑ Let the players who are subbing into the game know where they will likely play.
- ❑ Tell the team to go have fun!
- ❑ Other _____
- ❑ Other _____
- ❑ Other _____

From L. Blom and T. Blom, 2009, *Survival Guide for Coaching Youth Soccer* (Champaign, IL: Human Kinetics).

of rocks, holes, and debris. You should also check for sprinkler heads that may not have fully disengaged. Once you know the field is safe, then you can focus your attention on getting your players ready for the game. Make sure each player has the proper equipment and that it all fits.

After you have checked your players, get out the equipment in preparation for the warm-up. Contrary to popular opinion, kids in the younger age groups need only 5 to 7 minutes for warm-up, and the older kids can warm up for about 15 minutes. The warm-up should be short for three main reasons: (1) You do not want to get your players tired before the game; (2) children do not need as long as adults to warm up the body; and (3) you will be lucky to get players to arrive by game time, let alone 30 minutes early. Your goals for the warm-up are to establish good pre-exercise habits, decrease risk of injuries by getting the body physically warm and prepared, get players thinking about the game, and allow time for more touches on the ball.

When warming up for a game, you should first get the players' heart rates up with dynamic movement activities (see figure 10.4), then complete a stretching routine (see figure 10.5), and finish with a few activities

Figure 10.4 Dynamic Movement Activities

Each activity should be done for approximately 15 yards (14 m). Start players at a walking pace, and then increase the speed as they begin to get warmed up.

Activity	Description
Knees up	Players lift one knee at a time up toward the chest. Alternate sides as though they are marching.
Heels back	Players lift one heel at a time back toward the buttocks, switching from left to right.
Straight leg raise	Players extend one arm straight forward and try to swing the opposite leg up so the foot meets the hand. Switch to the opposite arm and leg.
Backpedaling	Players walk or jog backward, staying on their toes and leaning slightly forward.
Shuffling	Players move to the side, stepping with the lead foot first, following with the other foot. Players continue this movement without crossing their feet.
Skipping	Players skip while emphasizing the arm movement and focusing on skipping upward more than forward with the legs.
Jogging	To vary this activity, players can change direction and speed.

Figure 10.5 Stretching

Players should hold each stretch for 10 to 15 seconds. Repeat with both sides of the body if appropriate. Have players stretch only enough to feel mild tension, not pain. They should breathe slowly and evenly as they stretch. You may add other stretches, such as upper-body stretches for field players. Goalkeepers should spend an extra few minutes stretching their upper bodies.

Target of stretch	Description
Calf (back of lower leg)	Have players place their hands flat on the ground out in front of their bodies while keeping their heels on the ground. Their bodies should be at an angle (like an upside-down V or as if they are in the starting position to run a race), with the legs straight.
Hamstrings (back of upper leg)	Start with players sitting on the ground, with the soles of their shoes together tucked in toward the body. Then have them extend one leg in front and lean forward, reaching toward the foot of the extended leg.
Quadriceps (front of upper leg)	Have players lie on their sides with legs extended. Then have them pull the heel of the top foot, with the top arm, toward the buttocks. The players should try to keep their knees close together.
Groin (inside of upper leg)	Have players sit on the ground, putting the soles of their shoes together. Then have them push down slightly on their knees with their elbows.

that involve the soccer ball (see figure 10.6). Your warm-up, like practice, will include basic skill practice and stretching. Unlike practice, you do not want to spend time coaching, and you do not need a theme. You do want to allow players to work briefly on the main skills (dribbling, passing, receiving, and shooting) they will use in the game. Choose drills and activities that you have already introduced in practice and that involve constant movement for most players. Do not choose drills or activities in which one player performs the skill while others stand in line. At some point during the warm-up, make sure players take a bathroom break. If you forget this important task, you will regret it when you do not have enough players to start the second quarter because everyone is in the

Figure 10.6 Ball Activities

Perform one to three of these drills and activities for approximately 3 to 5 minutes each.

Drill or activity	Description
Sharks and minnows	See page 55 in chapter 3
Knockout	See page 57 in chapter 3
Intersection	See page 60 in chapter 3
Fast footwork skills	See pages 41-43 in chapter 3
Tunnel passing	See page 82 in chapter 4
No-hand catch	See page 84 in chapter 4
Add-on	See page 87 in chapter 4
Circle passing	See page 83 in chapter 4
Monkey in the middle	See page 86 in chapter 4
Check, pass, shoot	See page 107 in chapter 5
Race to the ball	See page 135 in chapter 5
1v1 to goal	See page 134 in chapter 6

bathroom. You may also want to be prepared to shuttle some kids to the bathroom at halftime.

Managing the Game Positively

Your behavior, both verbal and nonverbal, sets the stage for the game. Through your behaviors and your coaching talks, you can create a positive environment that allows the players to have fun while working hard. Let them know it's okay to take chances and make mistakes as long as they are trying. Make a point to interact with every player individually before and after the game. This could be something as simple as a high five or pat on the back. You might give some specific instruction for the match or feedback on a particular decision or play the player made. The easiest way to make a kid feel important is to give her your undivided attention.

Game-Time Coaching Behaviors

Although you may think you are helping your players by constantly yelling instructions to them while they are on the field, you may actually end up having a team of robots who are waiting on your command before moving. Because soccer is a free-flowing game, you must let the kids play. Figure 10.7 provides a checklist you can use to determine whether you are overcoaching your team. If you have several checkmarks in the "often" column or most of your checkmarks are in the "sometimes" and "often" columns, then you may want to rethink your coaching behaviors. You may be overcoaching and not letting the players truly be involved in the game. Remember, the most meaningful education comes when players figure the game out for themselves.

Pep Talks

You can use short pep talks to communicate with your players before, during, and after the game. You want to let them know you are on their side and appreciate their efforts. These talks are useful to remind the kids about what they have accomplished rather than to point out what they still have left to learn. Make pep talks brief and supportive.

Pregame Talk   Chances are, even if you didn't grow up playing soccer, you probably did play other sports. You may have even played at a pretty competitive level. As you consider all your coaching duties, the pregame speech is something most coaches either love or hate. For those of us who were brought up by fiery coaches with well-thought-out monologues, this may seem like the time to become Mel Gibson in *Braveheart* and send the troops into battle. But wait a minute. Your players aren't troops. In fact, some of them are as excited about which flavor drink box they will get after the game as they are about any one of the plays that will occur during the match. Shelve your Vince Lombardi routine and go with something short and sweet. If you feel apprehensive about what you are going to say, don't worry about it. Most of the kids will forget what you said before the whistle even blows.

Figure 10.7 Coaching Behaviors Checklist

Behavior	Frequency		
	Never	Sometimes	Often
My voice is strained after a game.			
My pregame and halftime talks have more emotional content than specific technical content.			
I use catch phrases like "Suck it up" and "No pain, no gain" to motivate my team.			
I am exhausted at the end of a game.			
I seem to repeat the same comments throughout the game.			
I give players strict instructions about what they can do, using words such as *never* and *always*.			
I am reluctant to let players make their own decisions during a game.			
I offer instruction to players throughout the entire game.			
We practice specific set plays for throw-ins, corner kicks, and free kicks every practice.			
I give general advice like "Work harder," "You can do it," "Kick it farther."			

Adapted, by permission, from D. Simeone, n.d., *The perils of overcoaching youth soccer.* [Online]. Available: http://www.fundamentalsoccer.com/members/Simeone.html [January 5, 2009].

From L. Blom and T. Blom, 2009, *Survival Guide for Coaching Youth Soccer* (Champaign, IL: Human Kinetics).

There are three parts to a good pregame speech:

1. **Give the players the lineup.** You may be tempted to give the lineup during the warm-up, but you'll likely have to remind a player or two again right before the game, so it's usually best to tell them right before they take the field.

2. **Provide no more than two or three points and reminders.** Be specific and brief. You might remind them to talk and listen to one another, follow their shots, or move into open spaces when they don't have the ball.

3. **Tell the players to have fun.** One of the last things you should tell the players before they take the field is to have a good time. That is, after all, why you are doing this. Sometimes that last-minute reminder is as important for the coach as it is for the players.

Halftime Talk

At halftime, you will have another formal opportunity to address your squad. Remember, this is also the only time they have to take a break, a physical *and* mental one. Allow them some time just to relax and not focus on the game. They also need time to get a drink of water or to have an orange slice or two. Your players need a little time that doesn't require concentration on the task at hand. The less you take from them here, the more they'll have left to give in the second half. However, this doesn't mean you need to let them be chatterboxes or slip into lots of silliness; remember you have some important items to communicate at halftime.

This is a good time to use the sandwich approach for feedback. Position your constructive criticism (which should be a brief statement about what you want them to do better next time, rather than what they did wrong last time) in between two slices of positive feedback. For example, "Great job hustling to get to the ball. Once we get it, let's try hard to pass to an open teammate. Keep up the hard work." Much like the pregame speech, short and sweet is typically the best route to take. The priorities here are to give the players time to get water and relax, and to allow you enough time to make any substitutions or position changes.

Postgame Talk

Emotions are high for everyone after a game, so it is important to debrief the players, even if it is just for a few minutes. You want to let them know that regardless of their performance, you are excited for them and appreciate their efforts, so do not let your emotions dictate your postgame talk. If your team exceeded your expectations and you are full of pride, you should use the following four-point postgame talk. If your team crumbled and seemed to forget everything you did in practice, you should follow the same four-point postgame talk.

1. Start with the question "Did you have fun?" (Remember, this is the most important goal.)

2. Tell them one thing they did well as a team. This is only one sentence long. For example, "Good work today staying in position."

3. Give a single statement about what they can do better next time. For example, you could say, "Next game we want to pass to our teammates more."

4. Tell them that you enjoy coaching them and you will see them at practice on (fill in the date).

Your postgame talk will be four sentences long; that is it. Do not include lengthy explanations of anything because their emotions are racing, and they will not remember much. Save your explanation for practice. After the four-point coaching talk, let them enjoy their snacks and visit with their teammates, friends, and families.

Player Challenges

Just when you think you have your players' personalities figured out, the games will start, and strangely enough you may have a few players with Dr. Jekyll and Mr. Hyde syndrome. Some players will be consistent in their personality from practices to games, but other players may surprise you for the better or unfortunately even for the worse. Some of your players may raise the following objections at game time:

• **"I'll just sit here on the bench."** The pressure of games, even if leagues and coaches try to minimize it, can really affect some players. Parents with video cameras, grandparents who make planned visits, special clothes (a uniform), and lots of people jumping up and down yelling and screaming are some of the unique characteristics of games that often affect players. Some players may love the idea of performing in front of the crowd, but many others will become uncharacteristically shy. Don't force this type of player to play. Let him take things at his own pace. If you force him onto the field, he will most likely cry and just stand still anyway. Ask him why he doesn't want to play and what you can do to help him be excited for the game. Talk to him about the importance of helping his teammates or how fun it will be to kick the ball. Focus on the aspects of the game that you know he will like from your experiences with him at practice. If it happens regularly, be sure to discuss the situation with his parents.

• **"I want to pick flowers while I play."** If you can find a safe place to let her pick flowers (off the field), then go ahead and let her pick. As we have mentioned before, rarely is it helpful to force a child to play.

Games are supposed to be fun, so if a child wants to practice but is not interested in the game, there is a reason that you want to further explore. See if you can find out what is going on, and then do what you can to make the situation more enjoyable for the child. Now if a child doesn't want to practice or play in games, then soccer is probably not the sport for her. This is the time to chat with the parents.

- **"I don't want to play that position."** You will have players who do not want to play the position that you assign them. Some will respectfully listen to your directions, enter the playing field, and as the game starts make their way over to the position they want to play. Others will throw temper tantrums to demonstrate their dislike for your decision. Their aversion to a particular place on the field may come from anxiety, instructions from Mom or Dad, an issue with a teammate, or some other random perception of the position. Whatever the reason, you will ultimately want to get all players to play a variety of positions, so just giving in to this player is not really the best answer. Here are some other options:

    - Explain the situation to him. Tell him that everyone gets a chance to play different positions, so sometimes he will not get to play his favorite spot, but at other times he will.

    - Ask him about his concerns. Ask what it is about the position he does not like.

    - Barter with him. You can negotiate that if he plays outside defender in the first quarter, then he can play forward in the next quarter.

    - Be the adult. Tell him that if he wants to play, then he will play the position you have assigned to him.

- **"I don't want to pass the ball."** A child with this attitude affects everyone, so you must take care of it. Now there may be a legitimate reason why she does not want to pass the ball, but that is still not acceptable behavior at the recreational youth level. On the other hand, you don't want to interfere with the development of her own individual skills or stifle her creativity. No matter how skillful a player is with the ball, she still needs to learn about passing and using teammates to beat opposing players. Talk with her about the importance of passing and reinforce the pass attempts she makes in practices and games. Let her see that she can get praise and credit for passing, just as she can with completing individual skills. If just talking to her does not work, give her goals or restrictions in practice to help her work on passing. For example, when your team does gamelike drills in practice, restrict her to touching the ball only two or three times before she has to pass. It may take some time to get her to pick up new, unselfish behaviors. Be patient but persistent and consistent.

- **"I'm afraid of the ball."** This poor player's worst nightmare is playing in goal. And if he is not in goal, he is still probably scared. He plans his escape route as soon as he thinks the ball might be traveling his way. The best way to deal with this characteristic is to work on receiving the ball with various parts of the body in practice. He may be hard to deal with in a game; to limit his contact with the ball, don't put him in the back third of the field. If he does receive the ball when on the field, repeatedly tell him how well he did (even if his performance was far from perfect!).

Team Challenges

Because game time is time to let the players play, there will be little you can do to change the way your team is playing. There are no time-outs, the breaks between quarters or halves are barely long enough to get off the field to get a drink, and the players are probably getting instructions from several different people, so you do not have much control over the game's events. However, there are a few team issues to try to change during the game.

- **Beehive soccer.** If your team (or the other team) is swarming around the ball like bees close to their hive, encourage the players to spread out. Use key phrases like "Move to open space" and "Find your position." Teams often start out playing like this and then begin to relax and spread out as the game goes on, so give them a few minutes to get going before you start yelling to them. On the other hand, if the kids persist in playing the entire game as swarming bees, just let them go. Work on passing and positions in practice the following week.

- **Boomball.** If your players are just kicking the ball as far and as hard as they can every time the ball comes near them, they are playing boomball. Encourage them to keep the ball on the ground and find a teammate to pass to instead. When a player does pass on the ground to a teammate, be sure to recognize her efforts out loud to reinforce her behavior. If the other team is playing boomball, you will probably feel a little frustrated and be tempted to play the same style. Resist it. Stick with your game plan because it will make your players better, and it is the right way to play soccer. Encourage your players to keep the ball on the ground, pass to their teammates, and let the ball do the work.

- **Overly competitive and distracting parents.** Parents can make or break a coach's experience, so it is important to get them following your philosophy from the beginning of the season. Encourage parents to let you do the coaching while they do the cheering. Remind them that if the players hear instructions from too many sources it can distract them, take the fun out of the game, and prevent them from learning how to make decisions on their own. Ask the parents to clap and say, "Good job," "Keep it up," "You can do it," "Nice pass (shot, defense)," and "Well done." Then after the game, suggest that the parents say three things: "I love you and love to watch you play," "Did you have fun?" and "What do you want to eat?"

• **Dealing with referees.** The referees are another game-time factor that you cannot control. Most of the referees will be inexperienced and may be only a few years older than your players. They are not getting paid very much and really have a tough job because no one is ever happy with the decisions they make. Just let this factor go. It is the one you have the least control over, and because your team is not playing for the World Cup, the referees really do not matter in the big picture. Expect them to miss calls, and just roll with it. You will enjoy the game much more if you do this.

Managing Postgame Details

The coach has responsibilities after the game as well, but they are minimal. The first thing you want to do is shake hands with opposing players and coaches. To do this, have your players line up on the sideline in front of your bench facing the other team's bench. Then ask them to hold out their right hands to the side. The other team is lined up as well, but facing your team. Have the teams walk toward each other, slapping (nicely) right hands. Essentially they are giving high fives to the other team. As they walk by each other, they should say, "Good game." After shaking hands with the opposing players, be sure that you shake hands with the coach and the officials.

Now for the best part of the game—running through the parent tunnel. This is a completely optional but very fun show of support for the kids. Be sure the parents know this routine before your first game so there is not an awkward lull at the end the game. Instruct the parents to form two lines facing each other. Then tell them to put their hands up in the air while leaning toward the person across from them, forming a tunnel of sorts. Once the kids have shaken hands with the opponent, let them run through the tunnel. Then they can return to the player sideline for the postgame talk.

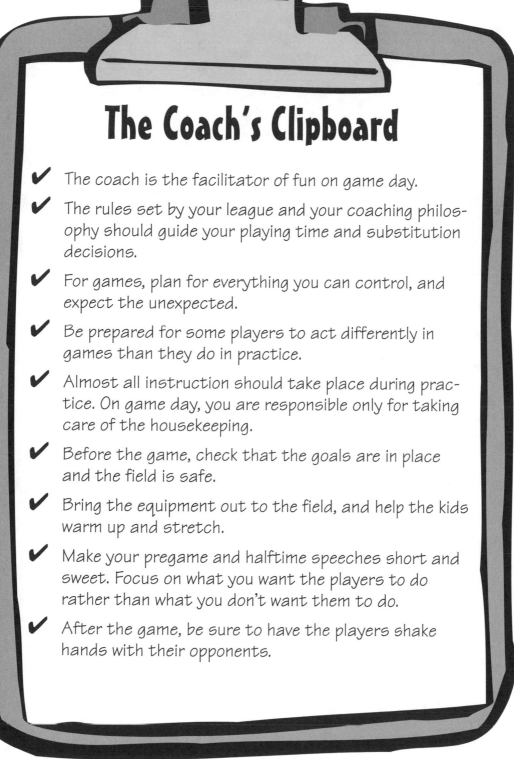

The Coach's Clipboard

✔ The coach is the facilitator of fun on game day.

✔ The rules set by your league and your coaching philosophy should guide your playing time and substitution decisions.

✔ For games, plan for everything you can control, and expect the unexpected.

✔ Be prepared for some players to act differently in games than they do in practice.

✔ Almost all instruction should take place during practice. On game day, you are responsible only for taking care of the housekeeping.

✔ Before the game, check that the goals are in place and the field is safe.

✔ Bring the equipment out to the field, and help the kids warm up and stretch.

✔ Make your pregame and halftime speeches short and sweet. Focus on what you want the players to do rather than what you don't want them to do.

✔ After the game, be sure to have the players shake hands with their opponents.

Off-Field Issues

We once saw a poster depicting the perfect soccer field. There was a long, long road leading through a sports complex, and next to the soccer field was a drop-off zone. There was no parking lot in sight. The idea is that the parents didn't have the option of staying to watch practice or coming to the games. The only ones on the field were the players and the coaches, and all that had to be done was to coach and play soccer. In a lot of ways, this does seem like soccer utopia. Show up at a specific time, set up the equipment, run through your seamless practice, and go home quietly. However, we all know there is much more to coaching than what happens on the field. What we want you to know is that some of that stuff is pretty fun, too.

Working With Parents

One of the biggest challenges for youth coaches may be parents. Parents may be too involved, not involved enough, critical, or worrisome. They may have lots of knowledge about the game and want to share it all with you, but they don't actually want to take on the responsibility of coaching. Alternatively, they may not really know anything about the game, but because their kid has played recreational youth soccer for three seasons, they may think they know enough to criticize you.

Criticism is likely to happen to every youth soccer coach. This happened to Lindsey and me shortly after I took over a U12 boys traveling team. I began to hear some grumblings that a few parents disagreed with my lineup. Several of the star players were now in positions that wouldn't garner as much spotlight as they had in the past, but I believed the players who had been up front would be more effective as defenders and outside midfielders. This left other players playing the forward positions and scoring most of the goals. I stressed during the introductory meeting that I would work to reinforce the importance of all the players and all the positions, but some of the parents hadn't completely bought my philosophy.

At our first home game of the season, Lindsey popped open a chair and sat quietly about 20 yards (18 m) down the sideline away from the parents. One mother, who was determined that I had already formed a vendetta against her child, began voicing her concerns to anyone who would listen (and some who wouldn't). During the course of the game, she slowly made her way down the sideline until she finally ran out of parents from either team. She eventually made her way to Lindsey, who the mother must have assumed was a new parent or had a child playing on the opposing team. With a variety of colorful words, the mother continued to explain what an idiot the new coach must be and questioned the club's decision to assign me to the team.

Lindsey encouraged her to speak to me after the game. She suggested that perhaps I could answer her questions or explain the thought process behind my decisions. Lindsey also pointed out that the son had started and played every minute of the game, and he seemed to be having fun. That point fell on deaf ears, and the mother reminded Lindsey that all coaches were arrogant jerks who wouldn't listen to a parent anyway. At that moment, the whistle blew, ending the match. Lindsey stood up, folded her chair, and politely said, "Well, then, maybe he will listen to me tonight at dinner."

Now, we are not trying to scare you, but we do want you to be prepared for the potential challenges. Although there are few perfect sport parents, you may have a team of very supportive, easygoing moms and dads. Most parents have very good intentions; they just may not be aware of how their behavior affects others. So spend your time on the parents who are supportive of their children and you, and be ready to search for the strengths of the challenging parents. The following types of parents are representative of those you might encounter, and the tips will help you bring out their strengths:*

- **Disinterested parents.** Disinterested parents are those who upset their children because they do not attend practices, games, or other team functions. There are many reasons why parents cannot attend functions, so do not assume the parents do not care about their children's activity. Instead, try to talk with them to let them know their participation is wel-

---

*Adapted from F.L. Smoll and S.P. Cumming, 2006, Enhancing coach–parent relationships in youth sports: Increasing harmony and minimizing hassle. In *Applied sport psychology: Personal growth to peak performance,* 5th ed., edited by J.M. Williams (New York: McGraw-Hill), 197-199.

come. You may need to give a little extra encouragement and support to the children who seem upset when their parents are not in attendance.

- **Overcritical parents.** Critical parents are those who spend an excessive amount of time scolding and berating their children's actions. You may hear them making threatening remarks before the game, critical comments at halftime, or judgmental commentary at the end of the game. These parents typically have unrealistic expectations for their children's performance and the parents' egos may be linked to this performance. A child's self-esteem is very vulnerable to adult comments and judgments, especially adults they respect, so critical parents can have a lasting negative effect on their child and others. They can also be hard to deal with, but it is worth your effort to talk with them about the benefits of using praise and encouragement to motivate and instruct athletes. Encourage the parents to create a supportive learning environment and to just let the kids play.

- **Sideline coaches.** Some parents, parents who have not accepted the responsibilities of coaching, spend the entire game offering instruction from the sideline. The comments coming from these parents are excessive, are often incorrect, may contradict your instruction, and can disrupt the players' concentration and the flow of the game. Game time is already a scary time for many athletes because of all the noise and people. The last thing the children need is to have multiple adults constantly offering instruction while they are trying hard to concentrate on making contact with a rolling ball. Sometimes parents get excited and think they are helping the children by directing their every move. They may not realize the effect their distracting and disruptive comments can have on children's performance and overall development. If you do have a parent who is coaching from the sideline, it is important to privately meet with him to discuss the concerns about sideline coaching from parents. If you are interested in having an assistant, you could always ask him to help you.

- **Overprotective parents.** Overprotective parents are those individuals who are worried about the physical contact that is part of the game of soccer. Typically these parents do not have much experience with soccer, so they are unfamiliar with the rules, regulations, safety measures, and typical injuries. They picture the worst-case scenario rather than the most common situations. Players will fall down, they will bump into each other, and they will kick each other, but soccer has been deemed a safe sport, where few severe injuries occur. If the environment is safe and the children are wearing the correct protective equipment, the benefits of participating (such as physical conditioning, team participation, and skill acquisition) far outweigh any potential risks. If you have a parent who is worried about the dangers of soccer, talk with her about her fears to see if the information you have about the game can help her relax. It may be worth having a league official meet with the parent as well.

Fun Extras

There is more to playing on a soccer team than just learning soccer. And your youth players know this better than any other group of competitive soccer players. Some of your players may even think these fun extras are more important than any soccer skill or drill. We have highlighted some of the extra things your players are hoping for this season.

Picture Day

With their angelic smiles, tucked-in shirts, and clean uniforms, you may not recognize your team on picture day. Your little soccer players may briefly turn into little models. Luckily, we have not heard of any player who did not return to his true self upon the completion of the picture session. Players and parents, and even coaches, want to remember their soccer experience from this season, and pictures are the best way to do that.

Typically, leagues schedule a picture day and teams are assigned time slots, so you will not have to do much planning or organizing—*just lots of reminding*! You will want to give several reminders through various methods of communication (at practice, at games, by e-mail, by phone, in a written note). You may also need to distribute order forms. Although you want to give parents some advanced warning about picture day, you do not want to hand out the forms until the last practice before the big day because they will often get lost in the household shuffle.

We have found it helpful to give the players (and parents) a meeting spot and ask them to arrive about 15 to 20 minutes before the assigned picture time. This gives the player who is always late a little breathing room and the player who always gets lost some time to find you. Once you have everyone there, you can do one last mirror check before heading over for the photo shoot.

End-of-Season Parties

Kids play soccer to have fun, be with their friends, and learn new skills. End-of-season parties meet two of these top three goals, and maybe all three depending on the type of party. So, an end-of-season party of some sort is another highlight for the kids. This get-together can be anything from having pizza at the field after the last game to a cookout and swimming party at a player's house. It does not matter what kind of party you have, just organize some type of last hurrah for the team and a chance for the players to hang out without having adults organizing their playful activities. It may be impossible to pick a date when everyone is able to attend (even if your team has only five players), but do try to identify a date early in the season so that families can make arrangements to attend if possible.

If you think you need to give a speech at the party, it can be short and sweet. Make it a "thank you" and "I had fun" speech. Be sure to thank your family, the people who helped out throughout the season, the parents for their support, and the players for their effort and hard work. You can include your favorite moment or a team highlight. Stay focused on the good moments; this is not a time to critique any situation or person.

Awards

Many leagues give participation awards in the form of trophies, plaques, or medals. Be sure to find out if your league does this so you can distribute them. If you have them in time for the end-of-season party, it is great to pass them out at that time. If not, you may need to have another brief meeting. Although the awards may not seem like much to us adults, the players love them (and some of their parents actually do, too). The parents and kids are proud of their accomplishments and enjoy the recognition, so we have found it ideal to pass awards out in front of all the players and parents. You can call each player up individually, say something positive and brief about him, shake his hand, give him the award, and let everyone clap. This is a nice final touch to the season.

Continuing Your Coaching Education

So you made it through the season without strangling Sarcastic Sandra (or arguing with her father). You defended your team's assigned practice area with courage and loyalty. And the time you spent analyzing playing time, lineups, and makeup-game schedules qualifies you for a management position in your company. Obviously, you are already looking forward to next season.

Every solid teaching philosophy and school district mission statement includes the phrase *lifelong learning*. This concept, while a little idealistic perhaps, is central to our growth as people and as successful members of whatever profession we claim. This certainly holds true for coaches. To fully appreciate the game and continue to contribute to the sport, it is important that coaches take on the responsibility of continuing education. You encourage the players to practice and improve between seasons, so you will want to do the same. Although there are many formal opportunities to learn and grow as a coach, there are also plenty of informal (and free) ways that you can continue your development.

Learn From Other Coaches

A great way to pick up new ideas for drills and practices is to watch other coaches working with their teams. If you have a few minutes before or after practice, watch what is happening on the field next to you. If you know of a particularly successful coach or if you have seen a team that impresses you, seek out a chance to watch them train. To get the very most out of the experience, talk to the coach in advance and ask to shadow him in practice. Asking to shadow a coach might sound a little awkward, but most of your colleagues would be happy to help a fellow coach and give back a little extra to the sport they love.

Stand with the coach so you can hear what he is saying to his players, and pick his brain about why he makes certain decisions on the field. Along with the actual drills that are being run, look for those little teachable moments and watch how he organizes his team. Transitioning from one drill to the next, introducing new topics, and closing the practice so the players leave with a clear message about what they have learned are all challenging issues that more experienced coaches have perfected.

Watch the Game

You can also learn by simply watching more soccer games. When your own team is on the field, you focus your attention on the specific concepts you have been working on in practice. You look to see if the kids are moving into space, picking their heads up while dribbling, and shooting with the instep. Maybe you have moved some players to new positions, so you are watching to see how they are responding.

What you probably aren't seeing clearly are the other aspects of the game that are going well or need extra work. By watching other teams play, you have the luxury of seeing the field from a different perspective. You don't have any decisions to make, so you can focus on any part of the game you wish. Maybe the defenders are especially well organized. You can watch how they move when they step to the ball and listen for what they are saying to one another or what instructions the coach is giving. When you identify what is working on the field, then you can start planning for how you might include those concepts in your own training.

You can also learn from college, professional, and international matches on television. Obviously, you won't expect your players to do everything you see those players doing, but there is still a lot you can take away from those games. There will certainly be one or two ideas you might stress to your players that are easier to see when watching the experts. Technical skills, such as taking a first touch away from pressure and shooting on the run, are easy to observe when watching the highest-caliber players. Movement without the ball, dropping the ball back to spread out the field, and combination play are examples of tactical concepts you might observe while watching a high-level match in person or on TV. Take what you see, and try to translate it into something your players can understand.

Be a Reflective Coach

Learning from other teams and coaches is great, but you can also learn a lot by reflecting on your own practices and games. Try to set aside a couple of minutes after a training session to jot down notes and make adjustments to your practice plan. If something worked great or if you ran a drill that the kids really got excited about, try to find another time and place to use it again. Likewise, when something just doesn't work at all, try to identify where the breakdown occurred. Is the drill too complicated, or could you have done a better job introducing it and explaining the steps? Is there too much standing around, or did you incorporate too many coaching points during the session? Did some other factor, such as weather, an impending birthday party, or another distraction, take away from the practice?

It is important that we, as coaches, be honest with ourselves about our own performance but also realistic about what we expect to get out of every practice. At the end of the day, our success is attached to the behavior and decisions that kids are making, so don't be too hard on yourself. Remember, if the kids are having fun, and if you are having fun, then you are on the right track.

Ask for Feedback

One of the very best measuring sticks is feedback from the parents and players. I know what you are thinking: *Do I want to know or am I supposed to care what the parents really think?* Keep in mind that this feedback isn't meant to direct every decision you make as a coach. You aren't going to ask for suggestions on what drills to run at practice, who should start the games, or where Little Ricky should be playing. The feedback you want is related to how the players feel about their soccer experience. Are they having fun? Do they look forward to practice and games? Do they think they are learning, being challenged, and improving their skills? This information won't affect what you are doing as much as it will affect how you are doing it.

Seek Out Other Soccer Resources

A number of resources are available for you to continue advancing as a soccer coach. In addition to this book, other coaching books, such as *Soccer Practice Games, 2nd edition,* by Joe Luxbacher and *Developing Youth Football Players* by Horst Wein, are widely available, and the number of credible Internet sites is growing every day. There are also videos available to offer support in almost every aspect of the game. Ask your local league officials and more experienced coaches about any tools they might be willing to share from their personal coaching library.

You can also grow a lot as a coach by attending a clinic. Your league may offer coaching clinics at the beginning or during the course of your season. If they don't, consider making that suggestion at a board meeting or coaches' function. Other clinics are offered through your state's youth soccer association. The National Soccer Coaches Association of America (NSCAA) and the United States Soccer Federation (U.S. Soccer) both offer formal training and licensure for coaches of every level.

Each organization has a specific curriculum that helps coaches train players from the earliest years of recreational soccer up until the collegiate and professional ranks. Every topic imaginable is covered, including first aid, age-appropriate fitness, and developing a coaching philosophy that fits your age group and competitive level. You will also leave with several new drills to use, and you'll find these classes to be a great place to network with other coaches at your level. Courses for beginning coaches typically last a few hours, and the cost is minimal. If you can't find a course in your area, recruit some of your colleagues. These organizations are typically more than happy to host a clinic if they have a group of coaches committed to attending.

Planning for Next Season

I once coached high school soccer with a guy who was great at looking ahead. With about two weeks left in the season, he was already mapping out the lineup for the following year. He took into account those who were graduating or moving away, and he planned adjustments that could be made with positioning of players. He even took into account those who might improve more than others because of summer camps or club soccer experiences. He spent a lot of time tinkering with who would be on the field and where they would be positioned. What he didn't always consider was what the team might do differently the next season or how he might adjust his approach to the game.

Unfortunately, in most recreational soccer leagues, teams do not necessarily stay intact from season to season. Players come and go, some move up in age group, and some will be placed on other teams. If you know you will be coaching most of the same players, then you can use the bridge philosophy in preparing for the next season. If you do not know your team's status or if you know you will not be coaching the same players, then you can use the self-refection philosophy.

Bridge Philosophy
On one side of the bridge is the current team. On the other side of the bridge is what you hope the next season holds. Picture what you would like your team to accomplish—not just wins and losses but also how the players will perform on the field. What individual skills would you like your players to learn or improve? Tactically, what concepts will you introduce or make a regular part of your team's play? Also consider any other changes you would like to make to the operation of the team. Is there any special equipment you would like to be able to use? Should you adjust the practice routine or add a tournament to the schedule? Do you want more help with the general operation of the team, such as adding a phone tree or e-mail bank, enlisting a social coordinator, or putting someone in charge of maps and directions?

With those ideas in mind, you begin to bridge the gap between where you are and where you are hoping to go. For the technical and tactical adjustments, attend a clinic if you can, search the Web, or talk with other coaches about what they are doing. Give your players some specific feedback, suggest skills they should work on before the next season begins, and encourage them to consider attending a clinic or two. And remind them that they don't need coaches and referees just to play soccer. They can get a lot out of putting together a pickup game with their friends and neighbors. As far as any equipment or housekeeping concerns, talk with some of the supportive parents about chipping in or taking on some extra responsibilities next season. Remind them that you can focus more on the coaching and the kids if you have fewer duties to worry about.

Self-Reflection Philosophy
If your role or your team personnel is going to change for the next season, then you do not want to spend much time focusing on the specifics of the past season or players. Instead,

focus on the overall experience that you, your players, and the parents had this year. Spend time reflecting on issues such as what worked well during practice, what you learned about this age group of players, and how you can more effectively organize practices and manage games. The basics of running a practice, preparing for games, dealing with different player personalities, handling parents, and coordinating off-field matters will be similar from team to team. The specifics will change, but you now have at least one season of experience to use as the backbone for the next one. Process what you would have changed as well as what went well. Then practice what you preached to your athletes; continue to practice or educate yourself to maintain or improve the skills you learned and be better for next year.

The Coach's Clipboard

✔ Dealing with some parents can be challenging. Try to communicate up front about your expectations for parent behavior.

✔ If a parent is creating a negative environment for a player or the team, have a meeting in private to discuss the situation.

✔ Picture day is a big day in the life of a youth soccer player. The league will schedule the time, but be sure to pass along this information and give reminders.

✔ An end-of-season party is a nice way to bring closure to the season.

✔ When distributing awards, call each player's name individually, and briefly remark on her contribution to the team.

✔ During the season and after the season is over, continue to improve your coaching by watching other coaches and games, reflecting on your coaching, seeking feedback, and seeking out other soccer resources.

🄯 About the Authors

Lindsey Blom has been involved in soccer for more than 20 years. As a former collegiate and semiprofessional player, she stays active in the game through coaching. She has coached boys and girls for more than 10 years at the recreational, select, high school, and state Olympic developmental levels. During her coaching tenure, she has teamed up with her husband, Tim, on many occasions. Their similar coaching philosophies yet different styles have allowed them to develop athletes who have gone on to compete in college. Lindsey currently teaches in the sport and exercise psychology program at Ball State University in Muncie, Indiana. She is a member of the National Soccer Coaches Association of America (NSCAA), carries a USSF D coaching license, and is a certified consultant through the Association for Applied Sport Psychology (AASP).

Tim Blom has had a unique opportunity to see, play, and coach soccer at a variety of levels over 25 years. Tim played soccer at Georgia Southern University at Statesboro, and his passion for the game led to his involvement in training and coaching. In Statesboro, he ran clinics for young recreational players, coached boys' and girls' club teams, and served as an assistant high school coach. He also served as the league development coordinator, overseeing player development and coaching education. He and his wife, Lindsey, worked together to win five West Virginia Club State Championships; they followed that with two more club state championships in Mississippi. Tim currently teaches mathematics and coaches the boys' soccer team at Eastwood Middle School in Indianapolis, Indiana. His coaching philosophy is based on teaching the life lessons of teamwork, sportsmanship, and hard work while always keeping soccer fun. Tim also has a USSF D coaching license and is a member of the NSCAA.

The Bloms reside in Indianapolis.